WeightWatchers®

cookeatenjoy

Tamsin Burnett-Hall

SIMON & SCHUSTER
A CBS COMPANY

First published in Great Britain by Simon & Schuster UK Ltd, 2007
A CBS Company
Copyright © 2007, Weight Watchers International, Inc.
Simon & Schuster UK Ltd, Africa House, 64–78 Kingsway, London
WC2B 6AH

Weight Watchers, **POINTS** and **Core Plan** are trademarks of
Weight Watchers International, Inc., and are used under its control
by Weight Watchers (UK) Ltd

Weight Watchers Publications Team: Corrina Griffin, Jane Griffiths,
Nina Bhogal, Nina McKerlie, Clair Smith and Kirsten Ware
Photography by Steve Baxter
Styling by Rachel Jukes
Food preparation and styling by Carol Tennant
Design and typesetting by Jane Humphrey
Printed and bound in China

A CIP catalogue for this book is available from the British Library

Pictured on the back cover, from top to bottom: Manhattan
seafood soup, page 48; gourmet pizzas, page 62; beef chow
mein, page 68; apple and apricot muffins, page 28; tiramisu,
page 200

 POINTS® value logo: You'll find this easy to read **POINTS**
value logo on every recipe throughout this book. The logo
represents the number of **POINTS** values per serving each recipe
contains. The easy to use **POINTS** Plan is designed to help you eat
what you want, when you want – as long as you stay within your
daily **POINTS** allowance – giving you the freedom to enjoy the
food you love.

You'll find this distinctive **Core™ Plan** logo on every
recipe that can be followed freely on the **Core Plan**. These recipes
contain only foods that form part of the **Core Plan**.

This symbol denotes a vegetarian recipe and assumes
that, where relevant, organic eggs, vegetarian cheese,
vegetarian virtually fat free fromage frais and vegetarian low fat
crème fraîche are used. Virtually fat free fromage frais and low fat
crème fraîche may contain traces of gelatine so they are not
always vegetarian. Please check the labels.

This symbol denotes a dish that can be frozen.

Recipe notes
Egg size: Medium, unless otherwise stated.
All fruits and vegetables: Medium sized unless otherwise stated.
Raw eggs: Only the freshest eggs should be used. Pregnant
women, the elderly and children should avoid recipes with eggs
which are not fully cooked or raw.
Recipe timings: Are approximate and meant to be guidelines.
Please note that the preparation time includes all the steps up to
and following the main cooking time(s).
Polyunsaturated margarine: Use brands such as Flora Light, St Ivel
Gold, Benecol Light and Tesco Healthy Living Olive spread
Rice: If following **Core Plan** remember to use brown rice. If using
white rice, remember to calculate the **POINTS** values.
Core Plan: If following **Core Plan** you have a limited allowance of
2 teaspoons of healthy oil a day (olive, sunflower, safflower,
flaxseed, rapeseed) to use in recipes as you choose.

contents

Enjoy a healthy lifestyle

Cook, Eat, Enjoy is the ideal book if you love food and want to eat wisely. This fantastic new cookbook is full of clear, easy to follow recipes, creating meals that you can enjoy with friends and family and still lose or maintain your weight. It has some contemporary twists on classic recipes and the mouth-watering photography is certain to inspire. It's been designed for you by the experts at Weight Watchers to work alongside the Weight Watchers programme. Whether you're following the **POINTS® Plan** or the **Core™ Plan** you'll find something to suit every occasion. The recipes are all quick and easy to make, perfect for your lifestyle and with lots of useful information with the **POINTS** values clearly shown on every recipe. Before long you'll discover how to enjoy eating delicious, vibrant, fresh tasting healthy foods and you'll soon see the positive results in your weight loss.

In this book you'll find new ways to cook favourite family recipes in a healthier fashion, changing the way that you cook without difficulty as well as providing plenty of exciting new dishes to delight your taste buds. And you won't have to spend hours in the kitchen. Whether you're an experienced cook or new to the kitchen, you'll soon realise that there's nothing complicated involved in creating appetising, nutritious recipes; the techniques used are all straightforward and there are handy hints and tips to make preparation easier. There are 150 recipes for you to choose from, all with a clear **POINTS** value, and half of which are suitable for the **Core Plan** with the distinctive logo by the title, so you can easily find the recipes that help you to follow your chosen food plan.

This book has a great chapter packed full of your foolproof favourites, recipes for simple sauces, dressing and preserves and then moves on to chapters covering all occasions from breakfasts and simple suppers to indulgent puddings and food for entertaining. Plus, of course, plenty of trusty favourites such as casseroles, pies and roasts that will keep the whole family happy and well fed, healthily.

Cook, Eat, Enjoy will not only inspire you to learn more about eating wisely, but you'll discover how planning ahead and making meal plans can be a valuable tool to keep your weight loss on track. Enjoy the results.

where would you be without them?

Whether you're a new cook or an experienced chef, it's vital to have a variety of simple cooking techniques and recipes at hand as the basis of your cooking repertoire. Simple sauces such as the Basic white sauce can be used as building blocks for more involved dishes such as Lasagne, while recipes such as Peppercorn sauce or Roasted pepper salsa dress up a simple piece of grilled fish or meat, adding a good deal more interest to your meal.

Homemade salad dressings such as Tomato and basil and Thai salad dressing can be whipped up in moments and taste so much fresher and more vibrant than bottled low fat versions. There are sauces to make the most of a quick pasta meal, and you'll also find favourite accompaniments such as All purpose gravy, Sage, onion and apple stuffing and Bread sauce, as well as a couple of low **POINTS** value sweet preserve recipes to brighten up breakfast time.

Basic white sauce

This is a simple way to make a smooth white sauce, which can be easily adapted to make cheese sauce or parsley sauce; see below for details. *Takes 10 minutes.*

25 g (1 oz) low fat polyunsaturated margarine
25 g (1 oz) plain flour
150 ml (5 fl oz) vegetable stock
150 ml (5 fl oz) skimmed milk
salt and freshly ground black pepper

● Place the margarine, flour, stock and milk in a small saucepan and place over a medium heat.
● Using a whisk or a wooden spoon, stir until the sauce becomes smooth and thickens as it comes to the boil.
● Reduce the heat and simmer for 3 minutes, while stirring, to cook out the raw flavour of the flour. Season to taste before using.

variations For a parsley sauce with the same **POINTS** value, simply stir in 2 tablespoons of chopped parsley and a squeeze of lemon juice. To make cheese sauce, add $^1/_2$ teaspoon Dijon mustard and 40 g (1$^1/_2$ oz) grated mature half fat cheese until melted. This will be 4 **POINTS** values per serving.

❋ Ⓥ
4 POINTS values per recipe
115 calories per serving
Serves 2

All purpose gravy

A delicious, all purpose gravy to serve with roasts, chops or bangers and mash. *Takes 10 minutes to prepare, 10 minutes to cook.*

low fat cooking spray
1 small onion, chopped finely
25 g (1 oz) plain flour
450 ml (16 fl oz) vegetable stock
1 tablespoon soy sauce
1 teaspoon tomato purée
freshly ground black pepper

● Spray a frying pan with low fat cooking spray and cook the onion for 6–7 minutes over a medium heat until browned and softened. Stir in the flour and cook for 2 minutes or until it turns light brown.
● Gradually blend in the stock, followed by the soy sauce and tomato purée. Bring to the boil, reduce the heat and simmer, covered, for 10 minutes. Season to taste with freshly ground black pepper.

❋ Ⓥ *vegan*
1 POINTS value per recipe
36 calories per serving
Serves 4

Bread sauce

This creamy sauce is a classic accompaniment to roast turkey at Christmas, but it's also wonderful with roast chicken (see page 196).

Takes 5 minutes to prepare + 30 minutes standing, 10 minutes to cook.

300 ml (10 fl oz) skimmed milk
$^1/_2$ onion, thickly sliced
8 black peppercorns
8 cloves
1 bay leaf
salt
60 g (2 oz) fresh white breadcrumbs
freshly ground nutmeg
freshly ground black pepper
1 tablespoon low fat soft cheese

● Place the milk, onion, peppercorns, cloves, bay leaf and a pinch of salt in a saucepan. Bring to a simmer then remove from the heat, cover and leave to stand for 30 minutes.
● Strain the milk into a clean pan and discard the flavourings. Stir the breadcrumbs into the milk, place over a very low heat and leave to swell, stirring occasionally, for 10 minutes.
● Add nutmeg and black pepper to taste, then mix in the low fat soft cheese just before serving.

❋ ⓥ
4 POINTS values per recipe
68 calories per serving
Serves 4

Sage, onion and apple stuffing

Serve these savoury stuffing balls as part of a Sunday roast, or alongside grilled pork chops or chicken for a weekday treat. *Takes 15 minutes to prepare, 25 minutes to cook.*

100 g (3$^1/_2$ oz) crustless bread (about 4 slices)
$^1/_2$ small onion, chopped roughly
1 apple, cored and chopped roughly
1 tablespoon fresh sage, chopped roughly, or
    1 teaspoon dried sage
4 thick low fat sausages
freshly grated nutmeg
salt and freshly ground black pepper
low fat cooking spray

● Preheat the oven to Gas Mark 5/190°C/fan oven 170°C.
● Tear the bread into rough pieces and place in a food processor. Whiz to coarse crumbs, then add the onion, apple and sage and whiz again until everything is finely chopped.
● Squeeze the sausages out of their skins and into the processor bowl, add the nutmeg and seasoning, then pulse until the mixture comes together.
● Shape into 18 stuffing balls and place on a foil-lined baking tray. Lightly mist the stuffing with low fat cooking spray then bake for 25 minutes until crisp and browned. Serve three balls of stuffing per person.

❋
9 POINTS values per recipe
102 calories per serving
Serves 6

Thai salad dressing

This fragrant Thai salad dressing is particularly good on a salad of thinly sliced cucumber and crisp lettuce. *Takes 2 minutes.*

1 tablespoon lime juice
1 tablespoon soy sauce
$1/_2$ teaspoon granulated sweetener
2 tablespoons cold water
$1/_2$ red chilli, deseeded and finely chopped
2 tablespoons freshly chopped coriander

● Simply stir the ingredients together in a small bowl. Set aside for a couple of minutes for the flavours to mingle before use, if possible.

Ⓥ *vegan*
0 POINTS values per recipe
22 calories per serving
Serves 2

Quick cook raspberry jam

There's no need to worry about complicated jam-making techniques and setting properties; this quick jam recipe couldn't be easier, tastes fabulously fresh and contains no hidden extras. *Takes 2 minutes to prepare, 20 minutes to cook.*

200 g (7 oz) fresh raspberries
200 g (7 oz) caster sugar

● Preheat the oven to Gas Mark 4/180°C/fan oven 160°C.
● Place the raspberries and sugar in separate shallow ovenproof dishes. Place in the oven for 20 minutes until the sugar is thoroughly heated through.
● Using oven gloves, pour the sugar into the raspberries, stirring with care.
● Pour the mixture into a clean dry jar, cover with a lid and leave to cool to room temperature. Store in the fridge for up to 3 weeks.

❄ Ⓥ *vegan*
12 POINTS values per recipe
43 calories per serving
Makes 20 heaped teaspoons (fills 1 x 350 g jar)
1 teaspoon per serving

Lemon and lime curd

Delicious on toast, this zingy citrus curd also makes a great filling for a sponge cake, or can be swirled through yogurt and topped with fresh fruit for a quick pud. Bear in mind that it will become firmer the longer it is stored. *Takes 15 minutes + cooling.*

2 medium eggs, beaten
60 g (2 oz) caster sugar
juice of 2 lemons plus 1 teaspoon lemon zest
juice of 1 lime
1¹/₂ teaspoons (half a sachet) lemon and lime sugar
   free jelly crystals

- Whisk the eggs, sugar, lemon zest, lemon and lime juice together in a medium heatproof mixing bowl.
- Sprinkle the jelly crystals into 150 ml (5 fl oz) boiling water then make up to 300 ml (10 fl oz) with cold water. Set aside.
- Sit the bowl over a pan of gently simmering water, making sure that the base of the bowl doesn't touch the water. Stir for 6–8 minutes until the curd has thickened and coats the back of a wooden spoon.
- Remove from the heat and stir in the made-up jelly, then strain the curd into clean jam jars. Cover with lids and cool to room temperature, then store in the fridge and use within 2 weeks.

❄ Ⓥ
6 POINTS values per recipe
13 calories per serving
Makes 35 heaped teaspoons (fills 2 x 350 g jars)
3 teaspoons per serving

Simple peppercorn sauce

Drizzle this creamy sauce over a grilled steak or pork chops – perfection. *Takes 8–10 minutes.*

2 shallots, chopped finely
low fat cooking spray
100 g (3¹/₂ oz) low fat soft cheese
100 ml (3¹/₂ fl oz) beef stock
1 teaspoon coarsely crushed peppercorns

- Cook the shallots in low fat cooking spray in a non stick pan for 3 minutes until softened and golden brown.
- Blend in the soft cheese, beef stock and peppercorns and simmer for 2 minutes until slightly thickened.

2¹/₂ POINTS values per recipe
60 calories per serving
Serves 2

Roasted pepper salsa

For a taste of summer all year round, spoon this colourful salsa over grilled chicken or fish. *Takes 10 minutes to prepare + cooling, 25 minutes to cook.*

1 red and 1 yellow pepper
100 g (3¹/₂ oz) cherry tomatoes, chopped roughly
1 tablespoon fresh basil, shredded
2 teaspoons balsamic vinegar
salt and freshly ground black pepper

- Preheat the oven to Gas Mark 6/200°C/fan oven 180°C.
- Put the peppers in the oven, directly on the oven shelf. Put a piece of foil on the shelf underneath to catch any cooking juices and keep the oven clean. Roast for 20–25 minutes until the peppers are blackened and blistered, then transfer to a bowl, cover and leave to cool.
- When the peppers are cool enough to handle, peel off the skins, scoop out the seeds, and cut the flesh into ribbons.
- Mix the roasted peppers back into the juices that will have collected in the bowl, then stir in the tomatoes, basil, balsamic vinegar and add seasoning to taste. Serve at room temperature for the best flavour.

Ⓥ *vegan*
0 POINTS values per recipe
29 calories per serving
Serves 4

Creamy white sauce

An alternative to a flour-based white sauce, this is brilliant for layering in lasagne, pouring over vegetable gratins or just tossing through cooked pasta. *Takes 5 minutes.*

100 g (3¹/2 oz) low fat soft cheese
60 g (2 oz) very low fat plain fromage frais
50 ml (2 fl oz) skimmed milk
¹/2 teaspoon Dijon mustard
salt and freshly ground black pepper

- Blend all the ingredients (except the seasoning) in a non stick saucepan, whisking until smooth.
- Heat gently until simmering and season to taste.

Ⓨ
3 POINTS values per recipe
73 calories per serving
Serves 2

Mayo replacement

A virtually fat free alternative to mayonnaise.
Takes 5 minutes.

60 g (2 oz) very low fat plain fromage frais
¹/4 teaspoon Dijon mustard
¹/2 teaspoon lemon juice
15 g (¹/2 oz) low fat soft cheese
salt and freshly ground black pepper

- Simply mix together all the ingredients, except the seasoning, until smooth and season to taste. Use within 2 days, stored in the fridge.

Ⓨ
¹/2 POINTS value per 2 tablespoons
11 calories per serving
Makes 4 tablespoons

Vegetable stock

Homemade stock vastly improves the flavour of soups and sauces for next to no effort. If you want to freeze stock without taking up too much room in the freezer, reduce the strained stock by boiling rapidly to give a concentrated stock that will need diluting before use. *Takes 5 minutes to prepare, 25 minutes to cook.*

1 onion, chopped roughly
1 leek, chopped roughly
2 carrots, chopped roughly
1 stick celery, chopped roughly
2 sprigs parsley
1 bayleaf
8 black peppercorns
salt

- Place all the ingredients in a large pan with a pinch of salt and 1.5 litres (2¾ pints) cold water.
- Bring to the boil, skim off any scum that rises to the surface, then simmer uncovered for 20 minutes.
- Strain and store in the fridge for up to 4 days.

❄ Ⓥ *vegan*
0 POINTS values per recipe
9 calories per serving
Makes 1.2 litres (2 pints)

Tomato and basil dressing

This fresh dressing is good on pasta salads or drizzled over steamed vegetables as well as on leafy salads. Use ripe tomatoes for a fully rounded flavour. *Takes 5 minutes.*

2 ripe tomatoes
½ small garlic clove, crushed (optional)
6 large basil leaves, shredded
½ teaspoon red or white wine vinegar
½ teaspoon tomato purée
salt and freshly ground black pepper

- Cut a cross in the base of each tomato, place in a bowl and cover with boiling water. Leave to stand for 1 minute, or until the skins loosen.
- Drain, then peel off the skins and roughly chop the flesh and seeds.
- Place in a blender with the remaining ingredients and whiz to a smooth purée. Add a little cold water to thin the dressing down if you wish. If you don't have a blender or food processor, chop the tomatoes finely and mash all the ingredients together with a fork.

Ⓥ *vegan*
0 POINTS values per recipe
16 calories per serving
Serves 2

Apple sauce

Serve warm or cold with sausages, roast pork or the Pork and Apple Meatloaf on page 102. *Takes 10 minutes to prepare, 5 minutes to cook.*

3 medium cooking apples, peeled, cored and sliced
6 cloves
1 tablespoon cider vinegar
1 tablespoon granulated artificial sweetener
     (optional)

● Place the apples, cloves and cider vinegar in a pan with 3 tablespoons water.
● Cover and cook over a medium heat for 5 minutes or until the apples break down. Stir until smooth then add the sweetener, if using. Remove the cloves before serving.

❄ Ⓥ *vegan*
2¹/₂ POINTS values per recipe
35 calories per serving
Serves 6

Quick tomato pasta sauce

A speedy fresh pasta sauce, you can use this as the basis for countless quick suppers (see below). Freeze extra portions for the nights you don't have time to cook from scratch. *Takes 15 minutes.*

1 medium red onion, chopped finely
2 garlic cloves, crushed
low fat cooking spray
500 g carton passata
1 tablespoon fresh thyme leaves or 1 teaspoon dried
salt and freshly ground black pepper

● In a non stick saucepan, fry the onion and garlic in low fat cooking spray for 2 minutes. Add 2 tablespoons water to stop the onion from sticking, cover the pan, and cook gently for 5 minutes or until softened.
● Stir in the passata, thyme and seasoning, then simmer the sauce for 5–6 minutes. Serve with pasta.

variations *Cacciatore sauce:* fry 3 rashers chopped back bacon and 140 g (5 oz) sliced mushrooms with the onion and garlic. This will be 1 **POINTS** value per serving.
Peperonata: add ¹/₂ each sliced red and yellow pepper at the start of the recipe and swap the thyme with fresh basil. The **POINTS** value will remain the same.

❄ Ⓥ *vegan*
0 POINTS values per recipe
37 calories per serving
Serves 4

get your
energy levels up

Breakfast is essential to kick-start your body into action each morning. Eating breakfast, even if it's just a speedy Strawberry and banana smoothie or Apple and apricot muffin on the run gets your energy levels up and provides you with the fuel your body needs to get you through until lunchtime. It helps to keep hunger at bay, so you can avoid reaching for an unhealthy mid-morning snack.

As well as quick Superfruits salad, Spiced raspberry and banana porridge or Overnight muesli to get you going, there are tempting recipes for weekend breakfasts and brunches for when you've got a bit more time such as Cinnamon French toasts with apricots and Potato pancakes with turkey rashers and tomatoes for when you fancy a cooked breakfast to fill you up from the start of the day.

Potato pancakes with turkey rashers and tomatoes

A tempting treat for a weekend brunch, these potato pancakes are also a healthy alternative to hash browns in a cooked breakfast. *Takes 20 minutes.*

1 medium egg, beaten
15 g (^{1}/$_2$ oz) self raising flour
225 g (8 oz) baking potato, peeled
salt and freshly ground black pepper
low fat cooking spray
4 turkey rashers
2 tomatoes, halved

- Preheat the grill.
- Mix the egg and flour together to form a batter.
- Coarsely grate the potato then squeeze out the excess moisture. Stir the potato into the batter and season generously.
- Lightly coat a non stick frying pan with low fat cooking spray then spoon the potato mixture into the pan as four separate pancakes. Cook over a medium heat for 3 minutes each side until golden brown.
- Reduce the heat, cover the pan and cook for 2 minutes more to cook the pancakes through.
- Meanwhile, grill the turkey rashers and halved tomatoes for about 5 minutes, or until cooked to your liking. Serve with the potato pancakes.

6 POINTS values per recipe
227 calories per serving
Serves 2

Breakfast muffin

A simply delicious fast fix to get you going in the morning. *Takes 5 minutes.*

1 English muffin, split
1 medium egg
low fat cooking spray
30 g (1^1/$_4$ oz) wafer thin smoked ham
1 tomato, thickly sliced

- Lightly toast the muffin and keep warm.
- Fry the egg in low fat cooking spray for 2 to 3 minutes, or until done to your liking.
- Pile the ham and tomatoes on to one half of the muffin, add the egg and the muffin top. Serve straightaway.

variations For a vegetarian alternative, replace the ham with a grilled flat mushroom. This will reduce the **POINTS** value to 3^1/$_2$.

4 POINTS values per recipe
267 calories per serving
Serves 1

Apple and apricot muffins

If you're short of time in the morning and need to grab breakfast on the run, make sure you've got a batch of these muffins stored in the freezer ready for an emergency fix. *Takes 12 minutes to prepare, 20–25 minutes to cook.*

low fat cooking spray
juice and grated zest of $^1/_2$ lemon
200 ml (7 fl oz) skimmed milk
300 g (10$^1/_2$ oz) self raising flour, sifted
1 teaspoon baking powder
salt
60 g (2 oz) caster sugar
100 g (3$^1/_2$ oz) dried apricots, chopped
1 apple, cored and diced
1 medium egg, beaten
80 g (3 oz) low fat polyunsaturated margarine

● Preheat the oven to Gas Mark 6/200°C/fan oven 180°C.
● Lightly grease a 12 hole muffin tin with low fat cooking spray, or line with paper muffin cases.
● Mix the lemon juice into the milk and set aside for 5 minutes to curdle. This will give the muffins a lovely light texture.
● Sift the flour, baking powder and a pinch of salt into a mixing bowl. Stir in the sugar, lemon zest, apricots and apple, then make a well in the centre.
● Pour the milk, egg and melted margarine into the bowl then stir briefly to mix into a batter. The batter should still look slightly lumpy, because if you overwork the mixture the muffins will be tough. Spoon into the muffin tin or paper cases then bake for 20–25 minutes until the muffins are well risen, firm and golden brown.

❋ Ⓥ
30$^1/_2$ POINTS values per recipe
158 calories per serving
Makes 12 muffins

Banana and honey crumpets

Popular with adults and children alike, these crumpets are terrific for an after work snack as well as for breakfast. *Takes 5 minutes.*

4 regular crumpets
30 g (1¼ oz) low fat soft cheese
1 medium banana, sliced
pinch mixed spice or cinnamon
1 heaped teaspoon honey

● Toast the crumpets under a preheated grill then spread with the soft cheese. Pile the banana slices on top, sprinkle with spice and return to the grill for 1 minute to warm through.
● Drizzle with the honey and eat straightaway.

Ⓨ
7¹/₂ POINTS values per recipe
261 calories per serving
Serves 2

Cinnamon French toast with apricots

A sweet version of eggy bread that's wonderful for a lazy weekend breakfast. *Takes 10 minutes.*

¹/₂ teaspoon ground cinnamon
2 teaspoons granulated artificial sweetener
2 medium eggs
2 tablespoons skimmed milk
3 medium slices wholemeal bread
low fat cooking spray
1 x 410 g can apricot halves in juice, drained
2 heaped tablespoons very low fat plain fromage frais

● Mix half the cinnamon with the sugar and set aside.
● Beat the remaining cinnamon together with the eggs and milk in a shallow dish. Cut the bread into triangles and dip into the egg mixture.
● Lightly coat a non stick frying pan with low fat cooking spray. Cook the eggy bread in two batches, frying over a medium heat for 1¹/₂–2 minutes each side until golden and crisp.
● Keep warm while you cook the second batch.
● Divide the French toast between two plates and sprinkle with the cinnamon sugar. Top with the apricots and fromage frais and serve immediately.

Ⓨ
8¹/₂ POINTS values per recipe
282 calories per serving
Serves 2

Spiced raspberry and banana porridge

A fantastic start for a cold day, this porridge is naturally sweetened by the addition of the delicious fruit. *Takes 5 minutes.*

40 g (1¹/₂ oz) porridge oats
150 ml (5 fl oz) skimmed milk
¹/₄ teaspoon ground cinnamon
1 small banana, sliced
40 g (1¹/₂ oz) raspberries

- Place the oats, milk and cinnamon in a non stick pan with 100 ml (3¹/₂ fl oz) cold water.
- Bring to the boil and simmer for 3 minutes or until thickened. Serve topped with the banana and raspberries.

Ⓥ
4 POINTS values per recipe
283 calories per serving
Serves 1

Overnight muesli

Oats make for a great breakfast as they provide slow-release energy throughout the morning. *Takes 5 minutes + overnight soaking.*

60 g (2 oz) porridge oats
1 apple, cored and grated coarsely
250 ml (9 fl oz) skimmed milk
to serve
2 heaped tablespoons 0% fat Greek yogurt
80 g (3 oz) fresh blueberries

- Place the oats in a bowl or plastic container, stir in the apple and milk, cover and leave to soak and soften overnight in the fridge.
- In the morning, top each bowlful with a heaped tablespoon of yogurt and the blueberries.

Ⓥ
6¹/₂ POINTS values per recipe
200 calories per serving
Serves 2

Vitality smoothie

This vegetable based smoothie is packed full of vitamins and antioxidants. *Takes 5 minutes.*

2 ripe tomatoes, chopped roughly
100 g (3^1/$_2$ oz) cooked natural beetroot, chopped roughly
zest and juice of ^{1}/$_2$ lemon
^{1}/$_2$ teaspoon grated fresh ginger
salt and freshly ground black pepper

● Blend the ingredients in a liquidiser until puréed. Alternatively, put the ingredients in a jug and purée with a hand held blender. Add a few ice cubes if you like. Serve immediately.

Ⓨ *vegan*
0 POINTS values per recipe
81 calories per serving
Serves 1

Berry blitz

If you've got a pack of summer berries in the freezer, you can whip up this smoothie even when there's no fresh fruit in the house, and there's no need to defrost them. *Takes 5 minutes.*

100 g (3^1/$_2$ oz) frozen summer berries
100 g (3^1/$_2$ oz) low fat strawberry or raspberry yogurt
150 ml (5 fl oz) skimmed milk

● Place all the ingredients in a blender and whiz until smooth and thick, or puree the ingredients in a jug using a hand held blender. Serve immediately.

Ⓨ
2^1/$_2$ POINTS values per recipe
124 calories per serving
Serves 1

Mango and melon smoothie

For a taste of the tropics, this smoothie can't be beaten. *Takes 5 minutes.*

1 large mango, peeled, stoned and chopped roughly
^{1}/$_2$ ripe melon, e.g. cantaloupe, galia or honeydew, peeled, deseeded and chopped roughly
juice ^{1}/$_2$ lime
4 ice cubes

● Blend the ingredients in a liquidiser until smooth, or puree the ingredients in a jug using a hand held blender. Pour into glasses and serve immediately.

Ⓨ *vegan*
3 POINTS values per recipe
120 calories per serving
Serves 2

Strawberry and banana smoothie

Whip up this smooth, creamy tasting smoothie for breakfast on the run. *Takes 5 minutes.*

1 ripe medium banana, sliced
150 g (5^1/$_2$ oz) ripe strawberries, trimmed and chopped roughly
100 ml (3^1/$_2$ fl oz) skimmed milk
^{1}/$_4$ teaspoon vanilla extract
2 ice cubes

● Place all the ingredients in a blender and whiz until smooth and frothy. Alternatively, put the ingredients in a jug and puree with a hand held blender. Serve immediately.

Ⓨ
2^1/$_2$ POINTS values per recipe
186 calories per serving
Serves 1

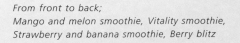

From front to back;
Mango and melon smoothie, Vitality smoothie,
Strawberry and banana smoothie, Berry blitz

Florentine mushrooms

A mouth-watering, vegetarian, cooked breakfast treat. *Takes 10 minutes.*

2 large flat mushrooms, stalks removed
low fat cooking spray
salt and freshly ground black pepper 100 g (3¹/₂ oz)
young leaf fresh spinach
1 tablespoon low fat soft cheese
1 medium egg

- Preheat the grill.
- Place the mushrooms in a baking dish, lightly coat with low fat cooking spray and season inside and out. Grill for 2 minutes, stalk side down, then turn over and grill for 2 minutes more, or until tender.
- Meanwhile, bring a pan of water to the boil for the poached egg and place the spinach in a separate saucepan. Cover and cook over a low heat until wilted. Stir in the cream cheese and seasoning, then keep warm.
- Break the egg into a cup. Use a spoon to create a whirlpool effect in the pan of boiling water, then slip in the egg. Reduce the water to a gentle simmer and cook for 2 minutes or until the egg is cooked to your liking.
- To serve, nestle the mushrooms side by side on a warm plate, and spoon the creamy spinach on top. Lift the egg out of the pan using a slotted spoon, and rest on top of the mushrooms. Serve immediately.

Ⓥ

2 POINTS values per recipe
162 calories per serving
Serves 1

Breakfast omelette

Save on the washing up with this one pan version of a cooked breakfast. *Takes 10 minutes.*

low fat cooking spray
80 g (3 oz) button mushrooms, quartered
5 cherry tomatoes, halved
2 medium eggs
salt and freshly ground black pepper

● Lightly coat a non stick frying pan with low fat cooking spray and cook the mushrooms for 2 minutes, then add the tomatoes.
● Beat the eggs with 1 tablespoon water and seasoning, then pour into the pan. Tip the pan from side to side to spread the egg around, then cook gently for 1$^{1}/_{2}$–2 minutes, or until set to your liking. Carefully fold over and serve on a warmed plate.

Ⓥ
2$^{1}/_{2}$ POINTS values per recipe
200 calories per serving
Serves 1

Superfruits salad

The fruits in this salad are bursting with antioxidants, which help to keep the body healthy and firing on all cylinders. *Takes 7 minutes.*

$^1/_2$ mango (150 g)
juice of $^1/_2$ lime
1 papaya, deseeded, peeled and chopped roughly
1 kiwi, peeled and cut into half moon slices
50 g (1$^3/_4$ oz) fresh blueberries

● In a blender (or in a jug with a hand held blender), purée the mango with the lime juice. Drizzle this over the other prepared fruits.

Ⓥ *vegan*
3 POINTS *values per recipe*
93 *calories per serving*
Serves 1

chapter three: **on the go**

For many lunch can be the trickiest meal to find an interesting solution for, especially as we don't always have the time either to prepare or to eat a meal in the middle of the day and there are so many obvious quick fix sandwiches available which can be high in **POINTS** values. So here is a range of tempting alternatives to transform lunchtimes – from Pastrami and sticky onion wraps to easily portable Pesto pasta salad and Chicken tikka in a lunchbox as well as a mouth watering Chilli tuna filling for a jacket potato or pitta bread. There's also an enticing range of hearty soups such as Chicken and corn chowder that can just as easily be served hot from a flask at work as from a pan on the stove at home. And don't forget, all these ideas are perfect for a light meal or a supper whenever you are short of time.

make the most of your time

Chilli tuna filling

Spoon this zingy tuna filling on to a crisp-skinned medium jacket potato or into a toasted pitta bread with crunchy salad leaves, either one for an additional 2¹/₂ **POINTS** values. *Takes 5 minutes.*

1 x 80 g can tuna in brine, drained
1 tablespoon low fat plain yogurt
1 tablespoon low fat mayonnaise
1 tablespoon sweet chilli sauce
1 tablespoon chopped fresh coriander
¹/₂ tablespoon lime juice
salt and freshly ground black pepper

● Flake the tuna into a bowl, add the remaining ingredients and mix well. Season to taste.

*2¹/₂ **POINTS** values per recipe*
166 calories per serving
Serves 1

Pastrami and sticky onion wraps

Fabulous for a lunch to take to work, wrap the filled tortillas in greaseproof paper or cling film to stop them from drying out. *Takes 10 minutes.*

1 onion, peeled
¹/₂ teaspoon olive oil
salt and freshly ground black pepper
2 soft flour tortillas
60 g (2 oz) low fat soft cheese
25 g (1 oz) wild rocket
4 slices pastrami

● Preheat the grill.
● Cut the onion into 10 or 12 wedges, slicing through the root so that the sections stay together. Place in a small roasting tin, drizzle with the oil and 3 tablespoons water, season and toss to coat.
● Cook under the preheated grill for 6–8 minutes, turning once. The liquid will evaporate, softening the onions as they cook. Meanwhile, gently warm the tortillas to soften them, either by dry-frying for 15 seconds each side, or by warming in the microwave for 15 seconds.
● Spread each tortilla with half the low fat soft cheese, then scatter on the rocket. Add the onions and two slices pastrami. Fold in one edge to form a base for the wrap, then roll up tightly.

*7¹/₂ **POINTS** values per recipe*
252 calories per serving
Serves 2

Curried chicken parcels

These spiced pasties are great for lunch or a snack.
Takes 25 minutes to prepare, 15 minutes to cook.

140 g (5 oz) carrots, peeled and diced
200 g (7 oz) potatoes, peeled and diced
low fat cooking spray
2 x 150 g (5$^1/_2$ oz) skinless chicken breast fillets, chopped finely
2 spring onions, chopped
50 g (1$^3/_4$ oz) frozen peas
1 tomato, chopped
2 teaspoons medium curry powder
salt and freshly ground black pepper
4 large sheets frozen filo, defrosted (each 26 x 48 cm)
1 tablespoon sunflower oil

● Preheat the oven to Gas Mark 5/190°C/fan oven 170°C. Add the carrots and potatoes to a pan of lightly salted boiling water, Cover and cook until tender, then drain. Meanwhile, lightly coat a non stick frying pan with low fat cooking spray, add the chicken and spring onions and stir fry over a high heat for 4 minutes, stirring to break up the chicken.
● Add the peas, tomato, curry paste and drained vegetables and fry for 2 minutes, lightly mixing the ingredients. Season and transfer to a plate to cool.
● Cut the sheets of filo in half lengthways, into 8 long strips. Working with one strip at a time, brush lightly with sunflower oil and spoon one eighth of the filling on the top. Bring the top left corner across to the other side to make a triangle. Fold the bottom of the pastry up and round until you have a triangular parcel. Place on a baking tray, greased with low fat cooking spray. Repeat with the rest.
● Bake for 15 minutes until crisp and golden brown. Serve warm or at room temperature.

❄
*12$^1/_2$ **POINTS** values per recipe*
152 calories per parcel
Makes 8 parcels

Pesto pasta salad

This veggie pasta salad is quick to make and can easily be prepared alongside your evening meal, ready to take to work the following day.
Takes 10 minutes.

40 g (1$^1/_2$ oz) mini pasta shapes, e.g. conghiglie or farfalline
60 g (2 oz) asparagus, chopped roughly
60 g (2 oz) broccoli, small florets
1 tablespoon pesto
$^1/_2$ red pepper, deseeded and diced
6 cherry tomatoes, quartered

● Cook the pasta, asparagus and broccoli in boiling water for 3–4 minutes, until the pasta is tender. Rinse in cold water and drain well.
● Mix together with the pesto, red pepper and cherry tomatoes.

Ⓥ
*3$^1/_2$ **POINTS** values per recipe*
282 calories per serving
Serves 1

3 1/2
POINTS
VALUE

Manhattan seafood soup

A meal-in-a-bowl type of soup, this makes for a hearty lunch or light meal. *Takes 15 minutes to prepare, 30 minutes to cook.*

2 rashers lean smoked back bacon, chopped
low fat cooking spray
1 onion, chopped finely
1 green pepper, deseeded and chopped
2 sticks celery, diced
700 ml (1^1/$_4$ pints) vegetable or fish stock
1 x 400 g can chopped tomatoes
300 g (10^1/$_2$ oz) potatoes, peeled and diced
400 g (14 oz) frozen mixed seafood selection,
    defrosted
salt and freshly ground black pepper

• In a large pan, fry the bacon in low fat cooking spray for 2 minutes on high heat until lightly browned.
• Add the onion, green pepper and celery and stir fry for 5 minutes, until beginning to soften. Add a splash of the stock if needed to stop the vegetables from sticking and scorching.
• Stir in the tomatoes, potatoes and stock.
• Season, cover, and bring to a simmer, then cook for 15–20 minutes or until the potatoes are tender.
• Stir in the seafood and heat for 2–3 minutes.
Ladle into warm deep bowls or mugs to serve.

NB If following the **POINTS** Plan, replace 100 ml stock with white wine for a richer flavour. The **POINTS** values remain the same for the serving, but for the recipe they will be 12.

11 POINTS values per recipe
174 calories per serving
Serves 4

Chicken and corn chowder

This chunky soup will fill you up fast. *Takes 10 minutes to prepare, 15 minutes to cook.*

1 x 150 g (5$^1/_2$ oz) skinless boneless chicken breast fillet, diced
low fat cooking spray
1 medium leek, trimmed, cleaned and chopped
salt and freshly ground black pepper
250 g (9 oz) potatoes, peeled and diced
425 ml (15 fl oz) chicken stock
100 g (3$^1/_2$ oz) baby corn, sliced
300 ml (10 fl oz) skimmed milk

- In a non-stick frying pan with a lid brown the chicken in low fat cooking spray over a medium heat for 2 minutes or until beginning to colour.
- Add the leek and seasoning, cover the pan, and cook for 2 minutes.
- Stir in the potatoes and stock, then simmer, covered, for 10 minutes.
- Mix in the corn and milk, return to the boil, and simmer for 5 minutes with the lid askew. Ladle into warm bowls to serve.

❄ *can be frozen without the potatoes or refrigerated for 3 days*
6 POINTS values per recipe
260 calories per serving
Serves 2

Chicken tikka lunchbox

A satisfying portable lunch that makes a great change from everyday sandwiches. *Takes 15 minutes, plus 30 minutes marinating.*

for the chicken tikka
3 tablespoons low fat plain yogurt
1 teaspoon medium curry powder
1 teaspoon tomato purée
1 x 100 g (3$^1/_2$ oz) skinless chicken breast
for the salad
40 g (1$^1/_2$ oz) brown basmati rice
1 teaspoon chopped fresh mint or pinch dried mint
5 cm (2 inches) piece cucumber, diced
$^1/_2$ yellow pepper, deseeded and diced
salt and freshly ground black pepper

- Mix together the yogurt, curry powder and tomato purée. Add the chicken breast, turn to coat and marinate for 30 minutes.
- Meanwhile cook the basmati rice in boiling water for 10 minutes, or until tender. Rinse in cold water, then drain well.
- Cook the chicken under a preheated grill for 10–12 minutes or until cooked through, turning half way through the cooking time. Cool and slice.
- Tip the rice into a bowl with the mint, cucumber and yellow pepper and mix together.
- Season to taste, then transfer to a lunchbox and top with the chicken tikka slices. Store in the fridge until ready to eat – it will keep for upto 2 days.

NB If you're following the **Core Plan**, make sure you use brown rice.

4$^1/_2$ POINTS values per recipe
318 calories per serving
Serves 1

Spicy squash and chickpea soup

A soup with an exotic hint of aromatic spices, and an interesting mixture of textures. *Takes 15 minutes to prepare, 30 minutes to cook.*

1 onion, chopped

low fat cooking spray

2 garlic cloves, crushed

1 red chilli, deseeded and diced

2 teaspoons ground cumin

1 teaspoon ground cinnamon

1 medium butternut squash, peeled, deseeded and chopped small

850 ml (1^1/$_2$ pints) vegetable stock

1 x 400 g can chopped tomatoes

1 x 410 g can chickpeas, drained and rinsed

salt and freshly ground black pepper

- In a large non stick pan, over a high heat, fry the onion in low fat cooking spray for 3–4 minutes, covered, until softened. Add a splash of the stock if needed to prevent the onion from sticking.
- Stir in the garlic, chilli and spices and cook for 15 seconds over a medium heat, then mix in the butternut squash and stir to coat in the spice mixture. Add 3 tablespoons stock, cover the pan and cook for 5 minutes over a medium heat.
- Pour in the remaining stock, the tomatoes, half the chickpeas and seasoning. Bring to the boil, cover and cook for 20 minutes or until the squash is tender.
- Cool slightly, then blend until smooth. Stir in the remaining chickpeas, adjust the seasoning and reheat gently until piping hot.

❄ Ⓥ *vegan*
4^1/$_2$ POINTS values per recipe
174 calories per serving
Serves 4

Sweet potato, leek and tomato soup

Sweet potatoes give this vibrantly coloured soup a fabulously velvety texture. *Takes 10 minutes to prepare, 20 minutes to cook.*

low fat cooking spray

2 medium leeks, trimmed, washed and chopped roughly

salt and freshly ground black pepper

400 g (14 oz) sweet potatoes, peeled and diced

1 x 400 g can chopped tomatoes

850 ml (1^1/$_2$ pints) vegetable stock

4 tablespoons very low fat plain fromage frais

2 tablespoons snipped fresh chives

- Lightly coat a large saucepan with low fat cooking spray, add the leeks and stir to coat. Season, and add 2 tablespoons water, cover the pan and sweat over a medium heat for 5 minutes until softened.
- Stir in the sweet potatoes, tomatoes and stock, bring to the boil and simmer, covered, for 15 minutes or until the sweet potato is soft.
- Cool slightly then blend until smooth. Adjust the seasoning if necessary and serve topped with a swirl of fromage frais and a scattering of chives.

❄ Ⓥ
6 POINTS values per recipe
139 calories per serving
Serves 4

Carrot and coriander soup

With a classic combination of flavours, this soup is a great way to fill up at the start of a meal without using any extra **POINTS** values. *Takes 10 minutes to prepare, 25 minutes to cook.*

1 onion, finely chopped
low fat cooking spray
2 teaspoons ground coriander
1 teaspoon ground cumin
750 g (1 lb 10 oz) carrots, peeled and chopped
900 ml (30 fl oz) vegetable stock
juice ¹/₂ lemon
salt and freshly ground black pepper
1 x 20 g pack fresh coriander, chopped roughly

- Over a medium heat, fry the onion in low fat cooking spray in a large covered pan with 2 tablespoons water, for 5 minutes, stirring once or twice.
- Add the spices and cook for 30 seconds, then stir in the carrots, followed by the stock. Bring to the boil and simmer, covered, for 25 minutes, or until the carrots are soft. Allow to cool slightly, then blend until smooth. Add the lemon juice and seasoning to taste, then finally stir in the fresh coriander just before serving.

❄ Ⓥ *vegan*
*0 **POINTS** values per recipe*
68 calories per serving
Serves 4

Smoked trout couscous salad

Smoked trout has a delicate flavour and texture that is complemented by the kick of the horseradish dressing. *Takes 10 minutes.*

100 g (3¹/₂ oz) plain couscous
salt and freshly ground black pepper
80 g (3 oz) low fat plain yogurt
2 teaspoons horseradish sauce
6 radishes, sliced into half moons
200 g (7 oz) cucumber, diced
1 spring onion, sliced
50 g (1³/₄ oz) watercress
125 g (4¹/₂ oz) smoked trout fillets, flaked

- Tip the couscous into a bowl, season, and stir in 150 ml (5 fl oz) boiling water. Cover and leave to stand for 5 minutes.
- To make the dressing, mix the yogurt and horseradish together and season.
- Stir the radishes, cucumber and spring onion into the softened couscous.
- Divide the watercress between two bowls and pile the couscous on top. Add the smoked trout and drizzle with the dressing just before serving.

*9¹/₂ **POINTS** values per recipe*
246 calories per serving
Serves 2

Falafel with minted yogurt

A good take-to-work lunch, these spiced chickpea patties can be served either warm or at room temperature on a bed of crisp lettuce, diced cucumber and tomato, with the minted yogurt drizzled on top. *Takes 15 minutes.*

100 g (3¹/₂ oz) low fat natural yogurt
¹/₄ teaspoon dried mint, plus a pinch extra
salt and freshly ground black pepper
1 x 410 g can chickpeas, rinsed and drained
1 teaspoon ground coriander
1 teaspoon ground cumin
1 medium egg white
2 spring onions, chopped
low fat cooking spray

- Mix the yogurt together with ¹/₄ teaspoon dried mint and seasoning, and set aside for the flavour to develop.
- Tip the drained chickpeas into a food processor, adding the extra pinch of dried mint, spices, egg white, spring onions and seasoning. Whiz until quite finely processed, but with a few chunky pieces of chickpeas remaining. Bring the mixture together in a ball, then shape into 8 small patties, using damp hands if the mixture is sticky.
- Preheat a non stick frying pan and mist with low fat cooking spray. Add the falafel and cook for 3 minutes each side over a medium heat until crisp and well browned. Serve with the minted yogurt.

❄ *falafel only* Ⓥ
5 POINTS *values per recipe*
180 calories per serving
Serves 2

Chickpea and tuna salad

A brilliant mixture of flavours, textures and colours, this filling salad looks just as good as it tastes. *Takes 20 minutes to prepare.*

1 red pepper, deseeded and quartered
125 g (4¹/₂ oz) green beans, trimmed and halved
juice ¹/₂ lemon
¹/₄ teaspoon ground cumin
¹/₄ teaspoon smoked paprika
salt and freshly ground black pepper
¹/₂ x 410 g can chickpeas, drained and rinsed
1 x 80 g can tuna in brine, drained
15 g (¹/₂ oz) wild rocket

- Preheat the grill to its highest setting.
- Place the pepper on the grill rack and cook for 8–10 minutes until charred. Transfer to a bowl, cover, and leave to cool slightly. When cool enough to handle, peel off the skin and roughly chop.
- Meanwhile, cook the green beans in boiling water for 3–4 minutes until tender. Drain and rinse in cold water to stop the cooking process.
- Mix the lemon juice, cumin, smoked paprika and seasoning together in a bowl. Add the green beans, chopped pepper, chickpeas and flaked tuna, and mix together well. Serve topped with the wild rocket leaves.

3¹/₂ **POINTS** *values per recipe*
300 calories per serving
Serves 1

Potato salad

A **Core Plan** version of potato salad in a creamy dressing, this main course sized version is livened up with the addition of chives and crispy bacon.
Takes 20 minutes.

400 g (14 oz) new potatoes, quartered
2 rashers lean back bacon
1 teaspoon Dijon mustard
50 g (1³/₄ oz) 0% fat Greek yogurt
50 g (1³/₄ oz) very low fat plain fromage frais
1 tablespoon snipped fresh chives
salt and freshly ground black pepper
1 Little Gem lettuce, leaves separated

● Cook the new potatoes in boiling water for 12–15 minutes until tender. Meanwhile, grill the bacon until crisp, then chop roughly.
● Mix the mustard with the yogurt, fromage frais, chives and seasoning in a large bowl. Drain the potatoes and cool for a couple of minutes before mixing with the dressing.
● Serve warm or cold, heaped on to the Little Gem leaves and scattered with the crispy bacon.

8 POINTS values per recipe
205 calories per serving
Serves 2

Tex mex tortilla

Bursting with flavour, this mouth-watering tortilla can be served warm from the pan, or left to cool and cut into wedges for a packed lunch.
Takes 20 minutes.

low fat cooking spray
1 small onion, chopped roughly
1 red and 1 green pepper, chopped roughly
2 garlic cloves, crushed
pinch crushed dried chillies
¹/₂ teaspoon ground cumin
4 medium eggs
salt and freshly ground black pepper
2 heaped tablespoons chopped fresh coriander

● Lightly coat a non stick frying pan with low fat cooking spray. Fry the onion and peppers for 5 minutes until browned, then stir in the garlic, chilli flakes and cumin, cover the pan, and cook for 2 minutes.
● Preheat the grill.
● Beat the eggs with seasoning and stir in the coriander. Pour over the vegetables and reduce the heat to low. Cook for 5 minutes until the bottom of the tortilla is set.
● Place the pan under the grill for 2 minutes to finish off the top, then serve, cut into wedges.

Ⓥ
5 POINTS values per recipe
232 calories per serving
Serves 2

chapter four: **quiet night in**

This chapter is all about finding speedy and delicious solutions to the ever-present question of 'what's for dinner?' The recipes are all quick to prepare, and the majority are on the table in between 10 and 30 minutes. There are plenty of low **POINTS** value variations on takeaway favourites like Thai prawn and vegetable curry, Beef chow mein and Gourmet pizza as well as speedy Summery prawn pasta, indulgent Rosemary lamb chops with ratatouille and Steak with sweet and sour onions. And the recipes are designed to feed just one or two people, they are perfect for a quiet night in on your own, or a romantic meal for two.

curl up
with a good recipe

Gourmet pizza

You can easily vary the basic pizza recipe here to add your favourite toppings to the uncooked pizza, but don't forget to adjust the **POINTS** values. Allowing the pizzas to rise before baking gives a thicker base that doesn't dry out during cooking.

Takes 15 minutes to prepare + 1 hour and 10 minutes rising, 15 minutes to cook.

150 g (5^1/$_2$ oz) plain flour

1 teaspoon fast action yeast

salt and freshly ground black pepper

1 teaspoon olive oil

1 x 230 g can chopped tomatoes

1 small garlic clove, crushed

1 tablespoon chopped fresh basil

100 g (3^1/$_2$ oz) cherry tomatoes, halved

80 g (3 oz) light mozzarella cheese, sliced

2 slices Parma ham, roughly torn

25 g (1 oz) wild rocket

● Reserve 1 tablespoon flour for kneading and rolling out, then sift the remainder into a mixing bowl.

● Stir in the yeast and ^{1}/$_2$ teaspoon salt, make a well in the centre and add the olive oil. Mix in around 100 ml (3^1/$_2$ fl oz) warm water, or enough to bring the mixture together to form a soft, but not sticky, dough.

● Turn out on to a floured surface and knead for 3 minutes until smooth. Return to the bowl, cover with cling film, and leave to rise in a warm place for 1 hour, or until doubled in size.

● Preheat the oven to Gas Mark 6/200°C/fan oven 180°C. Place the chopped tomatoes, garlic, basil and seasoning in a saucepan, simmer briskly for 5 minutes until thickened, then cool.

● Divide the pizza dough and roll out two bases, each measuring around 18 cm (7 inches) in

diameter. Transfer to a baking tray, spread with the tomato sauce, then scatter the cherry tomatoes and mozzarella on top. Leave to rise in a warm place for 10 minutes.

● Bake the pizzas for 15 minutes until well risen and crisp. Top with the torn Parma ham and rocket and serve immediately.

❋ *pizza bases covered in sauce can be frozen*
15 POINTS values per recipe
407 calories per serving
Serves 2

7 1/2
POINTS
VALUE®

Tuna burgers with cucumber relish

Tuna is a great storecupboard standby that's put to good use in these appetising burgers. Serve with a mixed leaf salad. *Takes 15 minutes.*

1 medium egg, beaten
2 tablespoons chopped fresh coriander
1 tablespoon sweet chilli sauce
1 spring onion, chopped finely
1 x 200 g can tuna in brine, drained and flaked
60 g (2 oz) fresh breadcrumbs
salt and freshly ground black pepper
low fat cooking spray
to serve
60 g (2 oz) cucumber, diced
$^1/_4$ yellow pepper, deseeded and diced
2 teaspoons seasoned rice vinegar
2 English muffins, split
2 lettuce leaves

- Mix the egg with the coriander, chilli sauce and spring onions then stir in the flaked tuna, breadcrumbs and seasoning.
- Mix together well and shape into two burgers, using damp hands to stop the mixture sticking.
- Lightly coat a non stick frying pan with low fat cooking spray. Fry the burgers for 4 minutes each side, until hot, crisp and golden brown.
- Meanwhile, mix the diced cucumber and pepper with the seasoned rice vinegar to make a crunchy relish.
- Lightly toast the English muffins and place half a muffin on each plate. Sit the burgers on the muffins, with a lettuce leaf tucked underneath. Spoon over the relish and top with the remaining muffin halves. Serve immediately.

❋ *burgers can be frozen before cooking, but not the relish or accompaniments*
11 POINTS values per recipe
379 calories per serving
Serves 2

Thai prawn and vegetable curry

A spicy, soupy curry that can easily be served as a meal in its own right. *Takes 15 minutes.*

200 g (7 oz) small new potatoes, quartered
100 g ($3^1/_2$ oz) green beans, trimmed and halved
150 g ($5^1/_2$ oz) button mushrooms, halved
low fat cooking spray
1 tablespoon Thai red curry paste
200 ml (7 fl oz) low fat coconut milk
1 teaspoon soft brown sugar
100 g ($3^1/_2$ oz) beansprouts, rinsed
200 g (7 oz) cooked peeled tiger prawns
juice $^1/_2$ lime
salt and freshly ground black pepper

- Cook the potatoes in boiling water for 7 minutes, then add the green beans and cook for a further 3 minutes. Drain and refresh in cold water to stop the cooking process.
- In a non stick saucepan, fry the mushrooms in low fat cooking spray, over a medium heat, for 2 minutes. Add the curry paste and fry briskly for 30 seconds before pouring in the coconut milk. Stir in the sugar, add the drained vegetables, and simmer for 1 minute.
- Mix in the beansprouts and prawns and simmer for 2 minutes until heated through.
- Add the lime juice and seasoning to taste, ladle into deep bowls, and serve.

11 POINTS values per recipe
305 calories per serving
Serves 2

Turkey steaks with caramelised apples

A really flavoursome dish of succulent turkey and golden apple wedges in a delicious sauce. Serve with green cabbage and 200 g (7 oz) potatoes, mashed with 2 tablespoons of skimmed milk, for an extra **POINTS** value of 2 per serving. *Takes 25 minutes.*

15 g ($^1/_2$ oz) low fat polyunsaturated margarine
1 tablespoon caster sugar
2 apples, cored and each cut into 6–8 wedges
low fat cooking spray
2 x 125 g ($4^1/_2$ oz) turkey breast steaks
1 small onion, chopped finely
salt and freshly ground black pepper
150 ml (5 fl oz) apple juice
1 tablespoon cider vinegar
50 g ($1^3/_4$ oz) half fat crème fraîche

- Melt the margarine and sugar in a large non stick frying pan, add the apple wedges and fry for about 3 minutes each side over a high heat until golden and lightly caramelised. Remove to a plate.
- Spray the frying pan with low fat cooking spray and season the turkey steaks. Fry for 3 minutes, then turn, scattering the onion around the turkey.
- Fry for a further 3 minutes, stirring the onion once or twice, then pour in the apple juice and cider vinegar.
- Bubble for 2 minutes, then stir in the crème fraîche and apples to warm through for about 30 seconds before serving.

$10^1/_2$ POINTS values per recipe
461 calories per serving
Serves 2

Malaysian chicken

Tantalise the taste buds with this deliciously different twist on chicken. Serve with 2 tablespoons of cooked rice for an extra $1^1/_2$ **POINTS** values, and a heap of steamed broccoli. *Takes 10 minutes to prepare, 12 minutes to cook.*

1 small onion, sliced
$^1/_2$ red chilli, deseeded and chopped finely
low fat cooking spray
1 x 150 g ($5^1/_2$ oz) skinless, boneless chicken breast fillet, diced
1 teaspoon light brown soft sugar
2 teaspoons soy sauce
4 tablespoons chicken stock or water
1 teaspoon rice vinegar or lime juice

- In a non stick saucepan, fry the onions and chilli in low fat cooking spray for 2 minutes.
- Add the chicken and stir fry for 1 minute over a high heat, then sprinkle in the sugar and cook for 1 minute more until caramelised.
- Mix the soy, stock and rice vinegar together. Pour over the chicken, cover the pan and simmer gently for 10 minutes.
- Remove the lid, increase the heat, and bubble for 2 minutes until slightly reduced, tossing the chicken in the sauce to glaze.

$2^1/_2$ POINTS values per recipe
211 calories per serving
Serves 1

Pork with five-spice plums

There's more than a hint of the Orient to this pan-fried pork dish. A medium portion (40 g/1^1/$_2$ oz) of egg noodles makes an ideal accompaniment, for an extra 2 **POINTS** values. *Takes 20 minutes.*

300 g (10^1/$_2$ oz) extra lean pork fillet
1 level tablespoon cornflour
^{1}/$_2$ teaspoon Chinese five spice powder
low fat cooking spray
1 tablespoon soy sauce
150 ml (5 fl oz) apple juice
1 garlic clove, crushed
2 tablespoons medium sherry
2 plums, stoned and each cut into 6 wedges
1 teaspoon redcurrant jelly

● Cut the pork into 15 mm (^{5}/$_8$ inch) slices.
● Mix the cornflour and five spice powder together and dip the pork in to coat lightly.
● Spray a non stick frying pan with low fat cooking spray, add the pork, and fry for 2–3 minutes each side until browned.
● Meanwhile, blend the remaining spiced cornflour with the soy, apple juice and 3 tablespoons of cold water, then set aside.
● Add the garlic to the pan and fry for 30 seconds without burning, then pour in the sherry and bubble briefly.
● Add the sauce mixture to the pan, add the plums and redcurrant jelly and simmer for 3 minutes, then serve.

*11^1/$_2$ **POINTS** values per recipe*
282 calories per serving
Serves 2

Beef chow mein

Chow mein dishes are a great way to prepare a complete well-balanced meal, all in one pan.
Takes 15 minutes.

60 g (2 oz) medium egg noodles
low fat cooking spray
125 g (4^1/$_2$ oz) lean stir-fry beef
4 spring onions, chopped roughly
60 g (2 oz) mange tout
80 g (3 oz) mushrooms, quartered
80 g (3 oz) beansprouts, rinsed
3 tablespoons oyster sauce
1 lime (optional)

● Cook the egg noodles in boiling water for 3 minutes until tender. Drain and rinse in cold water.
● Lightly coat a non stick frying pan or wok with low fat cooking spray. Stir-fry the beef and spring onions for 1^1/$_2$ minutes, then add the mange tout and mushrooms and cook for a further 1^1/$_2$ minutes.
● Mix in the beansprouts, noodles, oyster sauce and 1 tablespoon of water and heat through for 1–1^1/$_2$ minutes, stirring constantly. Serve immediately, squeezed with a little lime if you wish.

*7 **POINTS** values per recipe*
342 calories per serving
Serves 1

Vegetable fried rice

This multi-coloured, stir-fried rice dish is a great mixture of tastes and textures. Eating a good variety of differently coloured vegetables helps you to get a full range of nutrients. *Takes 15 minutes.*

60 g (2 oz) brown basmati rice
100 g (3^1/$_2$ oz) mushrooms, sliced
^{1}/$_2$ red pepper, diced
1 small courgette, diced
low fat cooking spray
4 spring onions, sliced
50 g (1^3/$_4$ oz) frozen peas
1 medium egg, beaten
salt and freshly ground black pepper

• Cook the rice in boiling water for 10 minutes, then rinse in cold water and drain well. Meanwhile, in a non stick frying pan, stir fry the mushrooms, pepper and courgette in low fat cooking spray for 4 minutes.

• Add the spring onions and frozen peas and cook for a further minute. Stir in the rice and cook for 1 minute, stirring.

• Beat the egg with seasoning, push the rice to one side of the pan, and pour in the egg. Cook for about 30 seconds until almost set, then stir into the rice and mix well, ensuring that the rice is hot.

NB If following the **Core Plan** make sure you use brown rice.

Ⓥ
5 POINTS values per recipe
390 calories per serving
Serves 1

Warm chicken and bacon salad

A fabulous combination of flavours, this warm salad is a great quick fix. *Takes 10 minutes.*

low fat cooking spray
salt and freshly ground black pepper
1 x 150 g (5^1/$_2$ oz) skinless boneless chicken breast fillet, diced
2 rashers lean back bacon, chopped
4 spring onions, chopped roughly
8 cherry tomatoes, halved
1 tablespoon balsamic vinegar
50 g (1^3/$_4$ oz) raw young spinach leaves or crispy salad leaves

• Lightly coat a non stick frying pan with low fat cooking spray.

• Season the chicken and add to the pan with the bacon. Stir fry for 5 minutes until browned.

• Mix in the spring onions and tomatoes and fry for 2 minutes, stirring occasionally. Add the balsamic vinegar and bubble for a few seconds, then immediately spoon over the salad leaves in a serving bowl so that they just begin to soften and wilt. Serve straightaway.

5^1/$_2$ POINTS values per recipe
287 calories per serving
Serves 1

Keema curry

Perfect for an easy Friday night supper served with a 150 g (5^1/$_2$ oz) portion of brown rice, green beans and a tablespoon of low fat plain yogurt for an additional 3^1/$_2$ **POINTS** values. *Takes 10 minutes to prepare, 30 minutes to cook.*

500 g (1 lb 2 oz) extra lean minced beef
1 onion, chopped finely
2 tablespoons medium curry powder
400 g (14 oz) potatoes, peeled and cut into 2.5 cm
    (1 inch) dice
200 ml (7 fl oz) beef stock
1 x 400 g can chopped tomatoes
salt and freshly ground black pepper
150 g (5^1/$_2$ oz) frozen peas

- In a large non stick pan, brown the mince and onion for 5 minutes, stirring frequently to break up the meat.
- Add the curry powder and potatoes and fry for 1 minute more.
- Pour in the stock and tomatoes, season, cover and simmer for 25 minutes.
- Finally, mix in the peas and cook for a further 5 minutes until tender.

❄

*24 **POINTS** values per recipe*
289 calories per serving
Serves 4

Summery prawn pasta

A zingy, fresh tasting pasta recipe that's packed full of nutrients – and tastes great. *Takes 15 minutes.*

125 g (4^1/$_2$ oz) pasta shells
150 g (5^1/$_2$ oz) broccoli, cut into small florets
150 g (5^1/$_2$ oz) sugar snap peas, halved
low fat cooking spray
1 garlic clove, crushed
4 ripe tomatoes, chopped roughly
zest and juice 1 small lemon
salt and freshly ground black pepper
200 g (7 oz) cooked and peeled prawns

- Cook the pasta in boiling water for 10–12 minutes, following pack instructions. Add the broccoli and sugar snap peas for the last 3 minutes of the cooking time.
- Meanwhile, lightly coat a saucepan with low fat cooking spray, add the garlic, and fry for 30 seconds without browning.
- Stir in the tomatoes, lemon zest, juice and seasoning, and cook for 2–3 minutes until the tomatoes have softened slightly. Stir in the prawns and heat through for 1 minute. Drain the pasta and vegetables then toss together with the sauce. Serve immediately.

*9^1/$_2$ **POINTS** values per recipe*
363 calories per serving
Serves 2

Mustardy pork and leeks

The delicious sauce from this one pan recipe is best spooned over a medium portion of brown rice, or served with mashed potato for an additional 2$\frac{1}{2}$ **POINTS** values. *Takes 15 minutes.*

low fat cooking spray
salt and freshly ground black pepper
1 x 150 g (5$\frac{1}{2}$ oz) pork loin steak
1 leek, trimmed, rinsed and chopped
100 ml (3$\frac{1}{2}$ fl oz) pork or chicken stock
2 teaspoons grain mustard
1 tablespoon low fat soft cheese
1 tablespoon very low fat fromage frais

- Lightly coat a non stick frying pan with low fat cooking spray.
- Season the pork steak, add to the hot pan and press down well. Fry for 4 minutes, then turn over and scatter the leek into the pan around the pork steak. Cook for a further 4 minutes, stirring the leek occasionally.
- Pour in the stock and add the mustard, then bubble the sauce rapidly for 2 minutes.
- Remove the pan from the heat and stir in first the soft cheese and then the fromage frais to enrich the sauce. Adjust the seasoning if needed before serving.

4 POINTS values per recipe
431 calories per serving
Serves 1

Shish kebabs with coriander relish

The fresh tasting, herby, yogurt relish provides a perfect accompaniment to these Indian-style lamb kebabs. Serve with a medium portion (150 g/ 5$\frac{1}{2}$ oz) of brown rice or bulgar wheat for an additional 3 **POINTS** values. *Takes 15 minutes to prepare, 10–12 minutes to cook.*

250 g (9 oz) lamb mince
$\frac{1}{2}$ small onion, grated
1 heaped tablespoon chopped fresh coriander
$\frac{1}{2}$ teaspoon ground cumin
$\frac{1}{2}$ teaspoon ground coriander
salt and freshly ground black pepper
for the relish
15 g ($\frac{1}{2}$ oz) fresh coriander, including the stalks, finely chopped
1 heaped tablespoon chopped fresh mint
$\frac{1}{2}$ small green chilli, deseeded and diced
1 tablespoon lemon juice
80 g (3 oz) low fat plain yogurt

- Preheat the grill, and line the tray with foil.
- Mix the lamb mince, onion, fresh coriander and spices together well, adding plenty of seasoning.
- Divide into 12 and shape into little sausages. Thread on to four metal skewers. Grill for 10–12 minutes, turning occasionally.
- Meanwhile, mix the chutney ingredients together, seasoning to taste. If you have a mini processor you can blitz them together to give a vibrantly green relish; otherwise, simply mix together in a bowl. Serve alongside the cooked kebabs.

11$\frac{1}{2}$ POINTS values per recipe
282 calories per serving
Serves 2

Rosemary lamb chops with ratatouille

The Mediterranean vegetable stew makes a colourful accompaniment to the grilled lamb chops. Serve with boiled new potatoes (150 g per person) for an additional **POINTS** value of 1^1/$_2$. *Takes 15 minutes to prepare, 15–25 minutes to cook.*

2 teaspoons chopped fresh rosemary
1 large garlic clove, crushed
salt and freshly ground black pepper
4 x 60 g (2 oz) lamb loin chops
for the ratatouille
low fat cooking spray
1 red onion, chopped roughly
1 yellow pepper, deseeded, and chopped roughly
1 courgette, roughly chopped
1 garlic clove, crushed
1 x 230 g can chopped tomatoes
1 teaspoon tomato purée

- Preheat the grill and line the pan with foil.
- Mix the rosemary, garlic and seasoning together, press on to both sides of the lamb chops and set aside for 10 minutes.
- Lightly coat a non stick saucepan with low fat cooking spray and cook the onion and pepper for 3 minutes.
- Add the courgettes and garlic and cook for 2 minutes then stir in the tomatoes, purée, seasoning and a splash of water.
- Cover the pan and cook gently for 15–20 minutes until the vegetables are tender. Meanwhile, grill the lamb chops for 12 minutes, or until cooked to your liking, turning half way through. Serve the chops on a bed of ratatouille.

11^1/$_2$ POINTS values per recipe
542 calories per serving
Serves 2

Steak with sweet and sour onions ✓ (6 POINTS VALUE)

The tangy sweet and sour onions make a delicious accompaniment to steak and creamy mashed potatoes enhanced with horseradish. *Takes 30 minutes.*

500 g (1 lb 2 oz) potatoes, peeled and chopped
    roughly
1 large onion, sliced
low fat cooking spray
250 ml (9 fl oz) beef stock
3 tablespoons sherry vinegar
$1^1/_2$ teaspoons granulated artificial sweetener
salt and freshly ground black pepper
2 x 125 g ($4^1/_2$ oz) sirloin steaks
4 tablespoons skimmed milk, warmed
$1^1/_2$ tablespoons horseradish sauce

- Cook the potatoes in boiling water for 20 minutes, or until tender.
- While the potatoes are cooking, fry the onion in low fat cooking spray for 5–6 minutes until browned, adding a splash of stock if needed to stop the onions sticking.
- Add the sherry vinegar, stock and sweetener to the browned onions, season and simmer uncovered for 10 minutes until tender and syrupy.
- Heat a non stick frying pan on the hob, season the steaks, and spray with low fat cooking spray. Cook for 3 minutes each side for medium steaks.
- When the potatoes are tender, drain into a colander. Use a potato ricer for the best possible texture, or mash as normal.
- Mix in the warmed milk, horseradish sauce and seasoning. Serve alongside the steak, with the sweet and sour onions spooned over.

$12^1/_2$ POINTS values per recipe
420 calories per serving
Serves 2

delicious and inspiring

chapter five: **veggie vitality**

Finding new and interesting ways to cook vegetables is a great way to ensure that you benefit from the full range of nutrients that these healthy choices have to offer. Vegetables are high in fibre and they will help to fill you up. In this chapter you'll find delicious accompaniments such as Mushroom and potato gratin and Courgette and feta fritters, main meal recipes like Leek and mushroom pie, Autumn vegetable stew and Aubergine parmigiana as well as a delicious vegetarian alternative to that old favourite Shepherd's pie – Cowboy pie.

Leek and mushroom pie

Crisp cheese and herb pastry acts as a delicious contrast to the flavoursome filling in this satisfying dish. The pie is great served with carrots and cabbage. *Takes 35 minutes to prepare, 30 minutes to cook.*

for the pastry

150 g (5^1/$_2$ oz) plain flour, sifted, plus 1 teaspoon for rolling

salt and freshly ground black pepper

80 g (3 oz) low fat polyunsaturated margarine

15 g (^{1}/$_2$ oz) freshly grated Parmesan

1 tablespoon freshly chopped thyme

for the filling

50 g (1^3/$_4$ oz) low fat polyunsaturated margarine

4 large leeks, trimmed, washed and sliced

300 ml (10 fl oz) vegetable stock

450 g (1 lb) mushrooms, quartered or halved

40 g (1^1/$_2$ oz) plain flour

300 ml (10 fl oz) skimmed milk

1 tablespoon grain mustard

● Preheat the oven to Gas Mark 5/190°C/fan oven 170°C.

● To make the pastry, sift the flour into a bowl with a pinch of salt and freshly ground black pepper. Rub in the margarine until the mixture is crumbly, then stir in the Parmesan and thyme. Add enough cold water to bring the pastry together into a smooth ball. Shape into a disc, wrap in cling film and chill for 30 minutes.

● To start making the filling, melt 2 teaspoons of the margarine in a non stick saucepan. Stir in the leeks and 2 tablespoons of stock, cover and cook for 5 minutes until tender, then transfer to a lipped ceramic pie dish.

● Put the mushrooms and 2 tablespoons of stock into the same saucepan and cook, covered, for 5 minutes. Lift the mushrooms into the pie dish using a slotted spoon, increase the heat under the saucepan and cook the remaining liquid for about 3 minutes until reduced by half, then pour into the pie dish.

● Now add the remaining margarine, stock, plain flour and milk to the saucepan. Bring to the boil, whisking until smooth. Simmer for 3 minutes then stir in the mustard and seasoning to taste. Pour over the leeks and mushrooms in the pie dish.

● Dust the work surface with 1 teaspoon flour and roll out the pastry thinly. Cut a narrow strip of pastry and press on to the rim of the pie dish. Brush with water, lift the pastry lid on top and press around the edge with a fork to seal the edges. Trim any excess pastry.

● Bake the pie for 30 minutes until crisp, golden and bubbling.

ⓥ

23^1/$_2$ POINTS values per recipe
392 calories per serving
Serves 4

Courgette and feta fritters

These melting cheese fritters evoke the feeling of a Greek island holiday. Just the thing for a light summery meal, or serve with a medium portion (150 g/5^1/$_2$ oz) of rice, for an extra 3 **POINTS** values. *Takes 15 minutes to prepare, 15 minutes to cook.*

75 g (2^3/$_4$ oz) plain flour
1 medium egg
4 tablespoons skimmed milk
salt and freshly ground black pepper
450 g (1 lb) courgettes, grated coarsely
75 g (2^3/$_4$ oz) feta, crumbled
low fat cooking spray
for the salad
^{1}/$_2$ cucumber, cut into chunky pieces
4 tomatoes, chopped roughly
^{1}/$_2$ red onion, sliced thinly
2 teaspoons freshly chopped mint

● Sift the flour into a bowl and beat in the egg, milk and seasoning to form a thick batter. Squeeze the excess moisture from the courgettes, then stir them into the batter, along with the feta.
● Lightly coat a non stick frying pan with low fat cooking spray. Cook the fritters in two batches; ladle six heaped spoonfuls into the frying pan and fry for 3–4 minutes on each side over a medium heat, until golden, crisp and cooked through. Keep warm while you cook the other six.
● While the fritters are cooking, simply mix the salad ingredients together, season and set aside until ready to serve with the hot courgette and feta fritters. Serve three fritters per person.

Ⓥ
12 POINTS *values per recipe*
63 *calories per serving*
Serves 4 *(makes 12 fritters)*

Butternut squash and goat's cheese strudel

Just the thing for a smart vegetarian main course.
Takes 40 minutes to prepare, 15 minutes to cook.

salt and freshly ground black pepper 600 g (1lb 5 oz) butternut squash, peeled, deseeded and diced
1 red pepper, deseeded and cut into 1 cm (^{1}/$_2$ inch) dice
low fat cooking spray
1 large leek, trimmed, washed and sliced
25 g (1 oz) pecans, chopped roughly
100g (3^1/$_2$ oz) soft rinded goat's cheese, diced
6 large sheets filo
to serve
150 g carton 0% fat Greek yogurt
1 small garlic clove, crushed
1 tablespoon snipped chives

● Preheat the oven to Gas Mark 7/220°C/fan oven 200°C. Season and mix the squash and red pepper, spread on a large baking tray, lightly coat with low fat cooking spray and roast for 10 minutes.
● Stir the leek into the vegetables and cook for a further 5 minutes, then add the pecans and cook for a further 5 minutes. Remove and cool slightly.
● Cut the sheets of filo in half to give 12 smaller rectangles. For each strudel, layer up three of these pieces, lightly coating with low fat cooking spray between each layer. Spoon a quarter of the vegetables on to each pastry rectangle, and divide the goat's cheese between them.
● Roll up into a log, tucking in the ends to hold in the filling. Transfer to a baking sheet, lightly mist with low fat cooking spray and bake for 15 minutes until crisp.
● Mix the yogurt with the garlic, chives and seasoning, and serve with the strudels.

❋ *before cooking* Ⓥ
18 POINTS *values per recipe*
284 *calories per serving*
Serves 4

Parsnip and cashew nut roast

Nut roasts are a bit of a veggie cliché but, properly prepared, they are positively delicious. Serve with zero vegetables and the All purpose gravy (page 8) for an extra ¹/₂ **POINTS** value per serving. *Takes 30 minutes to prepare, 1 hour to cook.*

low fat cooking spray
600 g (1 lb 5 oz) small parsnips, peeled and chopped
    roughly
25 g (1 oz) low fat polyunsaturated margarine
1 onion, chopped
100 g (3¹/₂ oz) cashew nuts
100 g (3¹/₂ oz) fresh breadcrumbs
1 medium egg, beaten
1 tablespoon freshly chopped thyme
grated zest 1 lemon + 1 tablespoon juice
salt and freshly ground black pepper

● Preheat the oven to Gas Mark 5/190°C/fan oven 170°C. Lightly grease a 900 g (2 lb) loaf tin with low fat cooking spray and line with baking parchment.
● Cook the parsnips in a pan of boiling water for 12 minutes until tender. Drain and mash. Meanwhile, melt the margarine in a saucepan with 2 tablespoons water. Add the onion and cook, covered for 5 minutes over a medium heat until soft.
● Grind the cashew nuts in a food processor, then mix with the breadcrumbs, egg, thyme, lemon zest and juice. Add the parsnips and onion and season. Pack into the lined tin and press down well. Cover with foil, lightly greased with low fat cooking spray.
● Bake in the oven for 45 minutes then remove the foil and bake for a further 15 minutes until brown and crisp on top. Let it sit in the tin for 15 minutes to firm up before turning out, so that it will slice more easily.

❄ Ⓥ
24 POINTS values per recipe
353 calories per serving
Serves 4

Aubergine parmigiana

Exudes the flavours of the Mediterranean. *Takes 30 minutes to prepare, 20–25 minutes to cook.*

1 aubergine, cut into 1 cm (¹/₂ inch) slices
salt and freshly ground black pepper
1 yellow pepper, quartered and deseeded
1 large courgette, cut into 1 cm (¹/₂ inch) slices
low fat cooking spray
400 g can chopped tomatoes
zest 1 lemon
1 tablespoon shredded fresh basil
125 g ball light mozzarella, sliced thinly
15 g (¹/₂ oz) freshly grated Parmesan

● Lightly sprinkle the aubergine slices with salt to draw out excess liquid. Set aside for 10 minutes.
● Preheat the grill to its highest setting and place the pepper and courgette slices under it. Lightly mist the courgettes with low fat spray, then grill for 5 minutes each side until golden. Grill the peppers for 8–10 minutes until the skins are charred.
● Transfer the courgettes to a plate. Place the peppers in a bowl, cover, and leave to cool, then peel off the skins. Pat the aubergine slices dry on kitchen paper and mist with low fat cooking spray. Grill for 3–4 minutes each side until browned.
● Meanwhile, preheat the oven to Gas Mark 6/200°C/fan oven 180°C. Make the tomato sauce by simmering the tomatoes, lemon zest, basil and seasoning for 6–8 minutes until slightly thickened.
● Spread half the tomato sauce in the base of a small baking dish and lay half of the aubergines on top. Cover with the courgettes and peppers, add the remaining aubergines and tomato sauce, followed by the sliced mozzarella and grated Parmesan. Bake for 20–25 minutes until bubbling.

Ⓥ
10 POINTS values per recipe
230 calories per serving
Serves 2

Chickpea and vegetable curry

A great panful of curry for feeding a crowd; the chickpeas really take on the spicy flavours of the sauce. Serve with a medium portion (150 g/5^1/$_2$ oz) of rice for an extra 3 **POINTS** values. Any leftovers taste even better the next day. *Takes 30 minutes.*

400 g (14 oz) potatoes, peeled and diced
2 large carrots, peeled and diced
250 g (9 oz) cauliflower, broken into florets
150 g (5^1/$_2$ oz) green beans, halved
1 onion, chopped
low fat cooking spray
2 tablespoons curry paste
400 g can chopped tomatoes
150 g (5^1/$_2$ oz) low fat plain yogurt
410 g can chickpeas, drained and rinsed
2 tablespoons freshly chopped coriander

● Cook the potatoes and carrots in a large pan of boiling water for 5 minutes. Add the cauliflower and green beans and cook for 5 minutes more, then drain the vegetables.

● Meanwhile, brown the onion in low fat cooking spray in a large pan, adding a splash of water if needed to stop it from sticking. Stir in the curry paste and cook for 1 minute, then add the tomatoes and yogurt.

● Mix the vegetables and chickpeas into the curry sauce and cook for 10 minutes. Serve topped with chopped coriander.

Ⓥ
12^1/$_2$ POINTS values per recipe
179 calories per serving
Serves 6

Summer vegetable fusilli

This vibrant pasta dish has a wonderfully fresh flavour, with a touch of creamy richness from the half fat crème fraîche. Serve with a large mixed salad. *Takes 20 minutes.*

300 g (10^1/$_2$ oz) fusilli pasta
150 g (5^1/$_2$ oz) green beans, halved
150 g (5^1/$_2$ oz) mange tout
2 courgettes, diced
low fat cooking spray
2 garlic cloves, crushed
salt and freshly ground black pepper
zest of 1 lemon, plus 1 tablespoon juice
4 tablespoons half fat crème fraîche
4 heaped tablespoons freshly chopped basil

● Cook the fusilli in a large pan of boiling water for 7 minutes.

● Add the green beans and cook for a further 3 minutes, then add the mange tout and cook for 2 minutes more, or until the fusilli is tender.

● While the pasta is cooking, fry the courgettes in low fat cooking spray in a non stick saucepan for 3–4 minutes until lightly browned. Stir in the garlic, 2 tablespoons water and seasoning, reduce the heat, cover and cook for 3 minutes or until tender.

● Drain the pasta and vegetables, reserving 4 tablespoons of the cooking water. Return to the pan and stir in the courgettes, lemon zest, juice, crème fraîche and basil, plus the reserved cooking water. Season well and serve in warmed bowls.

Ⓥ
20^1/$_2$ POINTS values per recipe
335 calories per serving
Serves 4

Creamy cauliflower and potato curry

An unlikely sounding recipe, but this is a case where the finished dish is so much more than the sum of its parts. The milk and tomato purée combine to give a silky textured spicy sauce, the flavour of which is taken on by the vegetables. *Takes 10 minutes to prepare, 15 minutes to cook.*

1 onion, chopped
low fat cooking spray
1 teaspoon cumin seeds
$^1/_4$ teaspoon ground turmeric
pinch hot chilli powder
2 tablespoons tomato purée
200 g (7 oz) potatoes, peeled and diced
200 g (7 oz) cauliflower, broken into florets
3 fresh tomatoes, chopped roughly
150 ml (5 fl oz) skimmed milk
salt and freshly ground black pepper
2 tablespoons freshly chopped coriander

- Fry the onion in low fat cooking spray for 3 minutes over a high heat until browned, then stir in the cumin seeds and cook for 30 seconds.
- Add the turmeric, chilli powder and tomato purée, then mix in the potatoes and cauliflower to coat in the spice paste.
- Add the chopped tomatoes, milk, 3 tablespoons cold water and seasoning. Bring to a simmer, cover and cook for 10 minutes.
- Remove the lid and cook for 5 minutes to reduce the sauce slightly. Serve with the coriander leaves scattered over the curry.

Ⓥ
2$^1/_2$ POINTS values per recipe
192 calories per serving
Serves 2

Cowboy pie

This hearty dish is a delicious vegetarian take on Shepherd's Pie. *Takes 20 minutes to prepare, 25 minutes to cook.*

1 onion, chopped
low fat cooking spray
200 ml (7 fl oz) vegetable stock
350 g pack Quorn mince
420 g can low fat, low salt baked beans
230 g can chopped tomatoes
salt and freshly ground black pepper
750 g (1 lb 10 oz) potatoes, peeled and cut into 5 mm ($^1/_4$ inch) slices

- Cook the onion in low fat cooking spray for 5 minutes until softened, adding a splash of vegetable stock if needed to prevent it from sticking.
- Stir in the Quorn mince, beans, chopped tomatoes and remaining stock, season, and simmer for 5 minutes, then pour into a baking dish.
- Add the sliced potatoes to a large pan of boiling water. Stir so that they don't stick together and cook gently for 4 minutes or until tender but not falling apart.
- Drain carefully and arrange on top of the mince mixture. Lightly mist with low fat cooking spray and bake in the oven for 25 minutes until the topping is golden and crisp.

Ⓥ
18 POINTS values per recipe
320 calories per serving
Serves 4

Three-bean chilli with wedges

A colourful pot of chilli that is full of goodness.
Takes 15 minutes to prepare, 25 minutes to cook.

1 onion, chopped
3 mixed peppers, deseeded and chopped roughly
low fat cooking spray
6 x 250 g (9 oz) medium size baking potatoes, cut
   into 8 wedges
1 vegetable stock cube
3 garlic cloves, crushed
$^1/_2$ teaspoon hot chilli powder
1 teaspoon ground cumin
$^1/_2$ teaspoon smoked paprika (optional)
410 g can kidney beans, rinsed and drained
410 g can flageolet beans, rinsed and drained
410 g can haricot beans, rinsed and drained
2 x 400 g cans chopped tomatoes
salt and freshly ground black pepper
150 g carton 0% fat Greek yogurt

- Preheat the oven to Gas Mark 7/220°C/fan oven 200°C. Cook the onion and peppers in a large pan, lightly coated with low fat cooking spray, for 7 minutes until softened and browned.
- Meanwhile, add the potato wedges and vegetable stock cube to a large pan of boiling water and cook for 5 minutes, until just tender.
- Drain into a colander then spread out on two baking trays and lightly mist with low fat spray. Place in the oven and cook for 20–25 minutes until crisp, turning half way through.
- Stir the garlic and spices into the onions and peppers, then add the beans, tomatoes and seasoning. Cover and simmer for 15–20 minutes.
- Ladle the chilli into bowls, top with a spoonful of yogurt and serve with potato wedges to dunk in.

❄ *chilli only* Ⓥ
28 POINTS *values per recipe*
373 calories per serving
Serves 6

Penne forestière

Dried porcini mushrooms intensify the flavour of this pasta sauce, giving it a wonderful richness. Use open cup mushrooms rather than button mushrooms if you can. *Takes 8 minutes to prepare, 12 minutes to cook.*

5 g ($^1/_4$ oz) porcini mushrooms, snipped
$^1/_2$ onion, sliced
low fat cooking spray
1 garlic clove, crushed
150 g (5$^1/_2$ oz) fresh mushrooms, chopped roughly
$^1/_2$ x 400 g can chopped tomatoes
salt and freshly ground black pepper
60 g (2 oz) penne

- Place the porcini mushrooms in a small bowl, cover with 4 tablespoons boiling water and leave to soak and soften.
- In a non stick saucepan, fry the onion in low fat cooking spray for 4 minutes, adding a splash of water if needed to prevent the onions from sticking.
- Stir in the garlic, fresh mushrooms and 2 tablespoons of the porcini soaking liquid, and cook for 3 minutes, then add the tomatoes, porcini and the rest of the soaking liquid. Season and simmer for 12 minutes.
- Meanwhile, cook the penne in lightly salted boiling water for 10–12 minutes until tender. Drain and mix with the sauce, then serve straight away.

❄ Ⓥ *vegan*
3 POINTS *values per recipe*
276 calories per serving
Serves 1

Autumn vegetable stew

This is based on a North American recipe called Three Sisters Stew, where the 'sisters' of the title were the ingredients found growing by early pilgrims: pumpkin, corn and beans. *Takes 15 minutes to prepare, 15 minutes to cook.*

2 onions, chopped roughly
2 red peppers, deseeded and chopped roughly
low fat cooking spray
450 ml (16 fl oz) vegetable stock
2 garlic cloves, crushed
1 teaspoon ground cumin
1 teaspoon ground coriander
pinch dried chilli flakes
750 g (1lb 10 oz) butternut squash, peeled, deseeded and chopped roughly
salt and freshly ground black pepper
410 g can pinto beans, rinsed and drained
150 g (5^1/$_2$ oz) frozen sweetcorn
juice 1 lemon
2 tablespoons freshly chopped coriander

- Cook the onions and peppers in low fat cooking spray for about 7 minutes until softened and browned, adding a splash of stock if needed to prevent them sticking.
- Stir in the garlic and spices, followed by the chopped squash, stock and seasoning. Cover the pan and simmer for 10 minutes.
- Stir in the pinto beans and sweetcorn, bring back to the boil and simmer for 5 minutes or until the squash is tender.
- Lift out some of the squash and mash roughly, then return to the casserole to thicken the sauce. Stir in the lemon juice and coriander just before serving, ladled into deep bowls.

Ⓥ *vegan*
5^1/$_2$ **POINTS** *values per recipe*
217 calories per serving
Serves 4

Mushroom and potato gratin

A fabulously rich and creamy potato gratin, this is great served with a lightly dressed mixed salad.
Takes 15 minutes to prepare, 1 hour to cook.

1 onion, sliced thinly
low fat cooking spray
225–250 ml (8–9 fl oz) vegetable stock
200 g (7 oz) open cup mushrooms, sliced
2 garlic cloves, crushed
100 g (3^1/$_2$ oz) low fat garlic and herb soft cheese
500 g (1 lb 2 oz) baking potatoes, peeled and sliced thinly
salt and freshly ground black pepper

- Preheat the oven to Gas Mark 4/180°C/fan oven 160°C.
- Cook the onion in a non stick saucepan, lightly coated with low fat cooking spray, for 2 minutes over a high heat.
- Add 2 tablespoons of the stock, cover and cook for 2 minutes, then stir in the mushrooms, garlic and seasoning, re-cover the pan and cook for 3 minutes. Remove from the heat and stir in the soft cheese and 3 tablespoons stock to make a sauce.
- Place half the mushroom sauce in the bottom of a lightly greased baking dish, then add half the potatoes, seasoning as you go. Repeat the layers of mushroom sauce and potatoes, season again and pour on enough vegetable stock to almost cover the potatoes.
- Cover with a sheet of lightly greased foil, place on a baking tray and cook in the oven for 45 minutes or until the potatoes are tender. Remove the foil and cook for a further 10–15 minutes to brown the top.

Ⓥ
8 POINTS values per recipe
300 calories per serving
Serves 2

Spinach and mushroom roulade

This recipe can be served as a main course with a hot tomato sauce and new potatoes, or it serves 6 people as a starter for 1½ **POINTS** values per serving. *Takes 30 minutes + cooling.*

low fat cooking spray 350 g (12 oz) fresh spinach
4 medium eggs, separated
freshly grated nutmeg
salt and freshly ground black pepper
350 g (12 oz) mushrooms, chopped roughly
2 garlic cloves, crushed
200 g (7 oz) low fat soft cheese
1 tablespoon skimmed milk
1 tablespoon snipped fresh chives

- Preheat the oven to Gas Mark 4/180°C/fan oven 160°C.
- Lightly grease a 23 x 33 cm (9 x 13 inches) Swiss roll tin with low fat cooking spray and line with baking parchment.
- Place the spinach in a large pan, without adding any liquid. Cover and cook for 2 minutes until wilted, then drain well squeezing out the excess liquid.
- Chop the spinach and place in a bowl, then mix in the beaten egg yolks. In a separate bowl, whisk the egg whites to the soft peak stage. Stir a spoonful of egg whites into the spinach to slacken the mixture then gently fold in the remainder, adding nutmeg and seasoning. Pour into the prepared tin and level the surface.
- Bake for 10–12 minutes until set and slightly springy to the touch. Turn out on to a sheet of baking parchment, leave the lining paper on and cover with a clean tea towel to keep the roulade moist as it cools.
- Meanwhile, lightly coat a pan with low fat cooking spray, add the mushrooms, garlic and seasoning, and cook, covered, for 3 minutes or until juicy.
- Uncover the pan and cook for a further 2–3 minutes until the juices have evaporated. Spread out on a plate and leave to cool. Mix the soft cheese with the milk and chives.
- Peel the lining paper away from the roulade and gently spread the cream cheese mixture all over.
- Scatter the garlic mushrooms on evenly, then, with a long side towards you, roll up the roulade, using the parchment to help you. Cut into slices to serve.

Ⓥ
*10½ **POINTS** values per recipe*
172 calories per serving
Serves 4

guaranteed to lift your spirits

chapter six: **comfort food**

Many of us have happy childhood memories of enjoying delicious and comforting meals like Macaroni and cheese or Toad in the hole. In this chapter you'll find healthy versions of these favourites which are perfect for those lazy days when you want to curl up and chill out. You'll also find old favourites like Beef cobbler, Sausage and bean hotpot and Bubble and squeak patties.

So whether you have had a busy or stressful day or just looking for something to remind you of those happy family memories there is something here that is guaranteed to lift your spirits.

Salmon and asparagus gratin

For a twist on this recipe, use lightly smoked fresh salmon fillets in place of regular salmon, for the same **POINTS** values. *Takes 15 minutes to prepare, 20 minutes to cook.*

25 g (1 oz) low fat polyunsaturated margarine
25 g (1 oz) plain flour
150 ml (5 fl oz) vegetable stock
150 ml (5 fl oz) skimmed milk
2 teaspoons lemon juice
salt and freshly ground black pepper
150 g (5^1/$_2$ oz) asparagus, chopped roughly
2 x 125 g (4^1/$_2$ oz) salmon fillets
2 teaspoons freshly grated Parmesan
1 tablespoon fresh breadcrumbs

- Preheat the oven to Gas Mark 6/200°C/fan oven 180°C.
- Place the margarine, flour, stock and milk in a small saucepan and place over a medium heat.
- Using a whisk or a wooden spoon, stir until the sauce becomes smooth and thickens as it comes to the boil.
- Reduce the heat and simmer for 3 minutes, then stir in the lemon juice and season to taste.
- While the sauce is cooking, simmer the asparagus in boiling water for 3 minutes or until just tender. Drain and place in the base of an ovenproof dish. Sit the salmon on top, then pour the sauce all over the fish.
- Mix the Parmesan and breadcrumbs together and scatter on top. Bake for 20 minutes until the topping is crisp and golden.

13 POINTS values per recipe
388 calories per serving
Serves 2

Macaroni cheese

A classic comfort food, this macaroni cheese is pepped up with the addition of tangy tomatoes and thyme. *Takes 15 minutes to prepare, 15 minutes to cook.*

125 g (4^1/$_2$ oz) macaroni
25 g (1 oz) low fat polyunsaturated margarine
25 g (1 oz) plain flour
150 ml (5 fl oz) vegetable stock
150 ml (5 fl oz) skimmed milk
salt and freshly ground black pepper
^{1}/$_2$ teaspoon Dijon mustard
40 g (1^1/$_2$ oz) grated mature half fat Cheddar cheese
1 teaspoon thyme leaves
6 cherry tomatoes, halved
2 teaspoons freshly grated Parmesan

- Cook the macaroni in a large pan of boiling water for 10 minutes or until just tender.
- Preheat the oven to Gas Mark 6/200°C/fan oven 180°C. Meanwhile, place the margarine, flour, stock and milk in a small saucepan and place over a medium heat. Season, then using a whisk or a wooden spoon, stir until the sauce becomes smooth and thickens as it comes to the boil. Reduce the heat and simmer for 3 minutes to cook out the raw flavour of the flour.
- Remove from the heat and stir in the Dijon mustard and the Cheddar cheese until melted. Drain the pasta and mix into the cheese sauce, then transfer to an ovenproof dish.
- Scatter the thyme, cherry tomatoes and Parmesan over the top and bake for 15 minutes until golden brown and crisp on top.

Ⓥ

13^1/$_2$ POINTS values per recipe
411 calories per serving
Serves 2

Pork and apple meatloaf

A mouth-watering meal that's great for when you are on a tight budget; serve with mashed potatoes, green vegetables and Apple sauce on page 22 or All purpose gravy on page 8, not forgetting to add the extra **POINTS** values. *Takes 10 minutes to prepare, 40 minutes to cook.*

25 g (1 oz) fresh breadcrumbs
2 tablespoons skimmed milk
450 g (1 lb) lean pork mince
1 small onion, grated
1 eating apple, cored and chopped finely
1 tablespoon freshly chopped sage or 1 teaspoon
    dried
salt and freshly ground black pepper

● Preheat the oven to Gas Mark 6/200°C/fan oven 180°C.
● Moisten the breadcrumbs with the milk in a mixing bowl.
● Add the pork mince, onion, apple, sage and seasoning, and mix together well.
● On a foil-lined baking tray, shape the mixture into a loaf measuring about 8 x 18 cm (3¹/₄ x 7 inches).
● Roast in the oven for 40 minutes. The juices from the meatloaf should run clear when the centre is pierced with a small skewer.
● Cut into eight slices and serve two per person.

❋
16 POINTS values per recipe
163 calories per serving
Serves 4

Mini toad in the hole

A fun way to serve up this family favourite; just add All purpose gravy on page 8 for an extra ¹/₂ **POINTS** value per serving, and your favourite zero vegetables. *Takes 15 minutes to prepare, 18–20 minutes to cook.*

1 tablespoon sunflower oil
12 thin, low fat sausages
1 large onion, sliced
125 g (4¹/₂ oz) plain flour
salt and freshly ground black pepper
1 medium egg
300 ml (10 fl oz) skimmed milk

● Preheat the oven to Gas Mark 7/220°C/fan oven 200°C.
● Divide the oil between the hollows in a 12 hole muffin tin (¹/₄ teaspoon in each) and heat in the oven for 2 minutes.
● Twist each of the sausages in half to form two cocktail sized sausages, and snip to separate.
● Place two sausages and some onion in each hollow and cook in the oven for 8 minutes until lightly browned.
● Sift the flour into a bowl, adding salt and freshly ground black pepper. Make a well in the centre, break in the egg, and gradually whisk in the milk to give a smooth batter. Transfer to a jug.
● When the sausages and onions are browned, pour in the batter, dividing it equally between the hollows. Return to the oven and cook for 18–20 minutes until the batters are risen, crisp and a rich golden brown. Serve three puddings per person.

variation For a vegetarian version, use eight veggie sausages, each cut into three chunks. Place two chunks in each hollow of the muffin tin and follow the rest of the method above.

18¹/₂ POINTS values per recipe
114 calories per serving
Serves 4 (makes 12 puddings)

Minced beef cobbler

The savoury scone-like cobbles that top this filling, family friendly dish mean that there's no need for extra potatoes. *Takes 25 minutes to prepare, 20 minutes to cook.*

1 onion, chopped
500 g (1 lb 2 oz) extra lean minced beef
1 tablespoon plain flour
300 ml (10 fl oz) beef stock
salt and freshly ground black pepper
250 g frozen mixed vegetables (carrots, peas and
　　sweetcorn)
150 g (5^1/$_2$ oz) self raising flour
60 g (2 oz) low fat polyunsaturated margarine
1 tablespoon freshly chopped thyme
80 g (3 oz) low fat plain yogurt
1 tablespoon skimmed milk

● Preheat the oven to Gas Mark 4/180°C/fan oven 160°C.
● Brown the onion and mince in a large pan for 8 minutes, then stir in the flour and stock. Season and simmer for 20 minutes, stir in the frozen mixed vegetables, then transfer to an ovenproof dish.
● For the cobbler topping, sift all but 2 teaspoons of the flour into a mixing bowl with a pinch of salt and a grinding of pepper. Rub in the margarine until the mixture is crumbly, then stir in the thyme and yogurt to make a soft, but not sticky, dough.
● Dust the work surface with the reserved flour and roll out the dough to a thickness of 1 cm (¹/₂ inch).
● Cut out 12 x 5 cm (2 inch) rounds using a cutter, re-rolling if necessary, and arrange on top of the mince. Brush with the milk and cook for 20 minutes until the cobbles have risen well and are cooked through.

*33^1/$_2$ **POINTS** values per recipe*
***401** calories per serving*
Serves 4

Maple and mustard chicken tray-bake

Great for a mid-week roast, this also cuts down on washing up as it's all cooked together in one tray. *Takes 15 minutes to prepare, 40 minutes to cook.*

800 g (1 lb 11 oz) small new potatoes, halved
2 red onions, chopped roughly
2 courgettes, chopped roughly
1 tablespoon olive oil
salt and freshly ground black pepper
4 x 125 g (4¹/₂ oz) skinless, boneless chicken breasts,
　　seasoned
2 tablespoons maple syrup
1 heaped tablespoon grain mustard
juice 1 lemon
250 g (9 oz) cherry tomatoes

● Preheat the oven to Gas Mark 6/200°C/fan oven 180°C.
● Parboil the potatoes in boiling water for 10 minutes. Drain and mix with the onions, courgettes, olive oil and seasoning in a large roasting tin. Place in the oven to cook for 15 minutes.
● Stir the vegetables around and add the seasoned chicken breasts to the roasting tin. Roast for a further 10 minutes.
● Mix the maple syrup with the mustard and lemon juice. Stir the vegetables around again, adding the tomatoes, and drizzle the maple mustard glaze all over the chicken and vegetables.
● Roast for a final 15 minutes.

*21 **POINTS** values per recipe*
***387** calories per serving*
Serves 4

Lamb stew with thyme dumplings

A British classic topped with fluffy herb dumplings, so you won't need extra potatoes to bulk out this meal. Serve with green cabbage. *Takes 30 minutes to prepare, 1½ hours to cook.*

salt and freshly ground black pepper
400 g (14 oz) diced lamb leg steak
low fat cooking spray
1 onion, chopped roughly
2 sticks celery, chopped roughly
600 ml (1 pint) lamb or vegetable stock
15 g (½ oz) plain flour
300 g (10½ oz) baby carrots
250 g (9 oz) swede, peeled and diced
1 large leek, sliced
for the dumplings
150 g (5½ oz) self raising flour
1 tablespoon freshly chopped thyme
1 tablespoon olive oil

- Preheat the oven to Gas Mark 2/150°C/fan oven 130°C.
- Season the diced lamb then lightly coat a casserole dish with low fat cooking spray. Brown the lamb in two batches over a high heat for about 4 minutes each, removing to a plate as it is done.
- Add the onion and celery to the casserole and brown for 5 minutes, adding a splash of stock if needed to prevent them from sticking.
- Stir in the flour then gradually blend in the remaining stock.
- Return the lamb to the casserole and mix in the carrots and swede. Bring to a simmer, cover, and cook in the oven for 1 hour.
- After 55 minutes, make the dumplings by sifting the flour into a mixing bowl, then stir in the thyme and olive oil, plus seasoning. Add enough cold water to bring the mixture together as a soft dough. Shape into eight dumplings.

- Mix the leek into the lamb stew and place the dumplings on top. Replace the lid and cook for 30 minutes longer.

❋
20 POINTS *values per recipe*
343 calories per serving
Serves 4

Sausage and bean hotpot

A hearty one pan recipe, this just needs some steamed broccoli or other green vegetable to accompany it. *Takes 10 minutes to prepare, 15 minutes to cook.*

low fat cooking spray
4 thick, low fat sausages
1 onion, sliced
1 garlic clove, crushed
$^1/_2$ teaspoon dried mixed herbs
$^1/_2$ x 400 g can chopped tomatoes
150 ml (5 fl oz) vegetable stock
1 x 410 g can cannellini beans, drained and rinsed
salt and freshly ground black pepper

- Heat the low fat cooking spray in a non stick frying pan and fry the sausages and onion for 5 minutes over a medium heat until browned.
- Add the garlic and herbs and cook for 30 seconds, then stir in the remaining ingredients. Bring to a simmer, cover and cook for 10 minutes.
- Remove the lid and cook for a final 5 minutes to thicken the sauce slightly.

variation For a vegetarian version, simply substitute four thick vegetarian sausages for the pork sausages for the same **POINTS** values per serving.

❁
8 POINTS values per recipe
294 calories per serving
Serves 2

Gammon hotpot

A warming hotpot of gammon and vegetables in a fragrant broth. *Takes 20 minutes to prepare, 40 minutes to cook.*

1 onion, cut into 8 wedges
2 sticks celery, chopped roughly
low fat cooking spray
650 g (1 lb 8 oz) gammon joint
3 medium carrots, peeled and cut into 4 chunks
6 potatoes, each around 100 g ($3^1/_2$ oz), peeled and halved
2 medium cooking apples, peeled and diced
2 sprigs fresh thyme
600 ml (1 pint) hot vegetable stock

- Preheat the oven to Gas Mark 2/150°C/fan oven 130°C.
- In a large casserole dish, brown the onion and celery in low fat cooking spray, frying for 8–10 minutes over a medium heat, adding a splash of water if needed.
- Nestle the gammon joint in the bottom of the casserole and add the carrots, potatoes, apples and thyme sprigs around the gammon.
- Pour in the hot stock, cover and bring to a simmer. Transfer to the oven and cook for 20 minutes, stirring the vegetables and turning the gammon joint over halfway through.
- When cooked, lift the gammon out on to a board and carve into slices. Ladle the vegetables and broth into deep bowls and top with the gammon. Serve three slices of the gammon per person, with the vegetable broth.

$41^1/_2$ POINTS values per recipe
440 calories per serving
Serves 4

One pot spicy chicken and rice

A simply scrumptious all in one rice dish that is a meal in itself. *Takes 20 minutes to prepare, 20 minutes to cook.*

low fat cooking spray
4 skinless chicken thighs, diced
1 onion, chopped roughly
1 yellow pepper, deseeded and chopped roughly
1 courgette, chopped roughly
2 garlic cloves, crushed
1 teaspoon paprika
pinch chilli flakes
1 teaspoon dried rosemary
175 g (6 oz) brown basmati rice
230 g can chopped tomatoes
salt and freshly ground black pepper
410 g can kidney beans, rinsed and drained

- Lightly coat a casserole dish with low fat cooking spray and brown the chicken for 4–5 minutes over a high heat. Transfer to a plate. Add the onion, pepper and courgette to the casserole and fry for 3 minutes.
- Stir in the garlic, spices, rosemary and rice and fry for 1 minute, then return the chicken to the casserole, add the tomatoes and 350 ml (12 fl oz) boiling water.
- Season well, bring to a simmer, and cover. Reduce the heat to a very low setting and cook for 15 minutes.
- Stir in the kidney beans and cook for a further 5 minutes.

NB Don't forget, if you're following the **Core Plan**, to use brown basmati rice.

variation Replace the chicken thighs with 350 g (12 oz) of chicken breast to reduce the *POINTS* values to $4^1/_2$ per serving.

22 POINTS values per recipe
364 calories per serving
Serves 4

Smoked haddock Florentine with chive mash

A real treat for one, this recipe can easily be doubled up to serve another person. *Takes 20 minutes.*

250 g (9 oz) potatoes, peeled and diced
150 g (5^1/$_2$ oz) smoked haddock, skinned
100 ml (3^1/$_2$ fl oz) skimmed milk
salt and freshly ground black pepper
low fat cooking spray
100 g (3^1/$_2$ oz) fresh spinach
1 tomato, deseeded and chopped
1 tablespoon snipped fresh chives
25 g (1 oz) low fat soft cheese

● Add the potatoes to a pan of boiling water, cover and cook for 12–15 minutes until tender.
● Meanwhile, place the smoked haddock in a pan with the milk and a grinding of pepper. Cover, bring to a simmer, and cook for 5–6 minutes until the fish flakes easily. Transfer to a plate and keep warm until ready to serve. Reserve the milk.
● Lightly coat a saucepan with low fat cooking spray, add the spinach, chopped tomato and seasoning and cook, covered, for 3–4 minutes until wilted. Keep warm until ready to serve.
● Drain the potatoes and mash with 1 tablespoon of the fish cooking milk. Stir in the chives and seasoning to taste.
● Whisk the soft cheese into the reserved milk to make a sauce and heat briefly to thicken. Season with pepper.
● Serve the haddock on a bed of the spinach and tomato mixture with the sauce spooned over and the mash on the side.

5 POINTS values per recipe
408 calories per serving
Serves 1

Orecchiette with pork ragù

Fennel seeds and chilli are key flavouring ingredients in traditional Italian sausages, which are often used for rich pasta sauces like this one. Shaped pasta such as orecchiette, which literally translates as 'little ears', catches the meat sauce so that it doesn't fall to the bottom of your bowl. *Takes 35 minutes.*

500 g (1 lb 2 oz) extra lean pork mince
2 large garlic cloves, crushed
^{1}/$_2$ teaspoon fennel seeds
^{1}/$_4$ teaspoon dried chilli flakes
1 tablespoon freshly chopped rosemary or 1 teaspoon dried
500 g carton passata
salt and freshly ground black pepper
225 g (8 oz) orecchiette (or any other pasta shape)
225 g (8 oz) broccoli, cut into small florets
50 g (1^3/$_4$ oz) very low fat plain fromage frais

● Dry fry the pork mince in a large non stick pan for 5 minutes, over a high heat, to brown. Add the garlic, fennel, chilli flakes and rosemary and cook for 1 minute.
● Stir in the passata and seasoning, cover, and simmer for 30 minutes.
● Cook the pasta in a large pan of boiling water, adding the broccoli for the last 3 minutes of the cooking time. Drain, reserving 100 ml (3^1/$_2$ fl oz) of the cooking water.
● Toss the pasta and broccoli with the sauce, stir in the fromage frais and reserved cooking water. Serve immediately in deep, warmed bowls.

❋ *meat ragù only*
27^1/$_2$ POINTS values per recipe
393 calories per serving
Serves 4

Stuffed chicken breasts

A simple, classic recipe that is wonderful served with Mediterranean style roasted vegetables, or just some grilled tomatoes. *Takes 10 minutes to prepare, 15 minutes to cook.*

50 g (1^3/$_4$ oz) smoked ham, diced
2 teaspoons snipped chives
salt and freshly ground black pepper
100 g (^{1}/$_2$ oz) low fat soft cheese
4 x 165 g (5^3/$_4$ oz) skinless, boneless chicken breasts
low fat cooking spray

● Preheat the oven to Gas Mark 6/200°C/180°C fan oven.
● Mix the ham, chives, and seasoning into the low fat soft cheese.
● Using a small sharp knife, make a pocket along the length of each chicken breast, taking care not to cut right through. Fill with the stuffing, then place the chicken breasts in a small roasting tin with a little low fat cooking spray.
● Roast for 15 minutes or until the chicken is cooked through; the juices should run clear when the thickest part of the chicken is pierced.

14 POINTS values per recipe
170 calories per serving
Serves 4

Beef stew

Smoked bacon really boosts the flavour of this tender braised beef stew. Serve over pasta, or with mashed potatoes for an extra **POINTS** value of 2^1/$_2$. *Takes 20 minutes to prepare, 1^1/$_2$ hours to cook.*

500 g (1 lb 2 oz) lean braising steak, diced
salt and freshly ground black pepper
low fat cooking spray
1 onion, chopped
4 rashers lean smoked back bacon, chopped
2 sticks celery, chopped roughly
2 large garlic cloves, crushed
400 g can chopped tomatoes
300 ml (10 fl oz) beef stock
200 g (7 oz) small mushrooms

● Preheat the oven to Gas Mark 2/150°C/fan oven 130°C.
● Lightly season the diced beef and brown in low fat cooking spray in a casserole, in two batches. Remove the meat to a plate as it is browned.
● Spray the casserole with a little more low fat cooking spray and cook the onion, bacon and celery over a high heat for 5 minutes.
● Stir in the garlic and cook for 30 seconds, then add the tomatoes, beef stock and browned beef.
● Season the stew, bring to a simmer, cover, and cook in the oven for 45 minutes.
● Stir the mushrooms into the stew, pushing them down into the liquid, then replace the lid and cook for a further 45 minutes or until the meat is tender.

❄
19 POINTS values per recipe
261 calories per serving
Serves 4

Marinated lamb with sweet potato cakes

An exotic tasting dish, imbued with the flavours of the Middle East. *Takes 35 minutes.*

600 g (1 lb 5 oz) lean lamb steaks
zest and juice $^1/_2$ lemon
1 red chilli, deseeded and diced
1 teaspoon ground cumin
1 clove garlic, crushed
salt and freshly ground black pepper
800 g (1 lb 11 oz) sweet potatoes, peeled and roughly chopped
3 tablespoons freshly chopped coriander
low fat cooking spray
150 g pot 0% fat Greek yogurt

● Mix the lemon zest and juice with half the chopped chilli, the cumin, garlic, and seasoning. Rub into the lamb steaks and set aside for 10 minutes.
● Preheat the grill.
● Cook the sweet potato in boiling water for 10 minutes or until tender. Drain and mash until smooth, then mix in the remaining chilli, seasoning and half the coriander. Spread out on a plate to cool for 5 minutes, then shape into 8 patties.
● Place the lamb on the grill pan and cook for 4–5 minutes each side, or until cooked to your liking.
● Meanwhile, lightly coat a non stick frying pan with low fat cooking spray, add the potato cakes and fry for 3–4 minutes each side over a medium heat until caramelised and crisp.
● Mix the remaining coriander and some seasoning into the Greek yogurt.
● Serve the lamb with the sweet potato cakes, topped with a dollop of the yogurt sauce.

25 POINTS values per recipe
366 calories per serving
Serves 4

Bubble and squeak patties

You can also use leftover cooked potatoes or mash for these crisp patties, which cuts down on preparation time. They are delicious served with a poached egg and two rashers of back bacon for $4^1/_2$ extra **POINTS** values. *Takes 25 minutes.*

500 g (1 lb 2 oz) potatoes, peeled and diced
4 spring onions, sliced
low fat cooking spray
100 g (3$^1/_2$ oz) cabbage, shredded
salt and freshly ground black pepper
1 medium egg, beaten

● Cook the potatoes in a pan of water for 10–12 minutes until tender. Drain and mash.
● Meanwhile, fry the spring onions in low fat cooking spray until they start to soften. Stir in the cabbage, seasoning and 3 tablespoons water. Cover the pan and cook for 4–5 minutes until tender.
● Mix into the mash, adding the beaten egg and seasoning to taste.
● Shape into six patties and fry, using low fat cooking spray, for about 3 minutes each side until golden and crisp. Serve immediately.

Ⓥ
7 POINTS values per recipe
248 calories per serving
Serves 2 (3 patties per person), or serves 3 as an accompaniment (2 patties per person) for 2$^1/_2$ POINTS values.

chapter seven: **party time**

It may be fabulous food for friends and family to celebrate a special occasion, or you are throwing a full blown party; whatever the event why not add a little luxury to special occasions with Tomato, thyme and goat's cheese tartlets, Smoked salmon bites, Marinated prawns in lettuce boats or Citrus crusted salmon. You're certain to find something that's a little bit out of the ordinary like Hallowe'en hubble bubble casserole, and you won't need to forsake your weight-loss goals. When food tastes this good, everyone can enjoy the feast.

enjoy the company

Sausage rolls

Always a popular item at parties, these sausage rolls will disappear fast when served warm from the oven. *Takes 15 minutes to prepare + chilling, 20 minutes to cook.*

250 g (9 oz) plain flour
salt and freshly ground black pepper
125 g (4$^1/_2$ oz) low fat polyunsaturated margarine
8 thick, low fat sausages
1 onion, grated
1 teaspoon grain mustard
1 tablespoon skimmed milk to glaze

- Reserve 1 tablespoon of flour for rolling out the pastry, then sift the remainder into a bowl with a pinch of salt.
- Rub in the margarine until the mixture is crumbly, then add just enough cold water to bring the pastry together. Wrap in cling film and chill for 30 minutes.
- Split the skins and then squeeze the sausage meat out and mix with the onion, mustard, and seasoning.
- Dust the work surface with the reserved flour and roll out the pastry to a rectangle measuring around 24 x 37 cm (9$^1/_2$ x 14$^1/_2$ inches). Cut into two long strips and add the sausage meat filling down the length of each piece of pastry. Dampen the edges with water and roll the pastry around the filling, pressing to seal.
- Slice each long roll into eight pieces and place on a lightly greased tray. Brush with milk and bake for 20 minutes until golden brown and crisp.

❄

33 POINTS values per recipe
116 calories per serving
Makes 16

Tomato, thyme and goat's cheese tartlets

These bite-sized tartlets are very moreish, and will soon disappear at a party. The recipe uses the individual kind of goat's cheese that has a soft edible white rind like Brie. You can also use the same quantity of crumbled feta cheese for $^1/_2$ **POINTS** value per tartlet. *Takes 15 minutes to prepare, 15 minutes to cook*

2 large sheets frozen filo pastry, defrosted
low fat cooking spray
150 g (5$^1/_2$ oz) cherry tomatoes, halved
100 g individual goat's cheese, diced
1 tablespoon freshly chopped thyme
1 medium egg, beaten
125 ml (4 fl oz) skimmed milk
salt and freshly ground black pepper

- Preheat the oven to Gas Mark 4/180°C/fan oven 160°C.
- Layer up the filo sheets, misting with low fat spray in between. Cut into eighteen 8 cm (3$^1/_4$ inch) squares and press into the hollows of two lightly greased mini muffin tins. Bake for 3–4 minutes until crisp and golden.
- Divide the goat's cheese, cherry tomatoes and thyme between the pastry cases, then mix the egg and milk together with seasoning and carefully pour into the tartlets.
- Bake for 13–15 minutes on the centre shelf until the filling is set. Carefully remove from the tin and serve warm.

Ⓥ

13 POINTS values per recipe
40 calories each
Makes 18

Goat's cheese and chive dip with cucumber sticks

Soft goat's cheese has a very mild flavour, so don't be scared to give it a go in this creamy dip.
Takes 5 minutes.

300 g (10^1/$_2$ oz) soft goat's cheese
150 g (5^1/$_2$ oz) low fat plain yogurt
1 garlic clove, crushed
2 heaped tablespoons snipped chives
freshly ground black pepper
2 large cucumbers, cut into batons

- Simply mix the goat's cheese with the yogurt, garlic, chives and freshly ground black pepper and spoon into a small serving bowl.
- Surround with the cucumber sticks for dipping.

Ⓨ
17^1/$_2$ POINTS values per recipe
211 calories per serving
Serves 8

Hallowe'en hubble bubble casserole

This sausage casserole is a popular choice for feeding a crowd of friends in cold weather. *Takes 15 minutes to prepare, 20 minutes to cook.*

low fat cooking spray
16 thick low fat sausages
6 rashers lean back bacon, chopped
2 x 415 g can reduced sugar and salt baked beans
1 x 400 g can chopped tomatoes
1 tablespoon Worcestershire sauce
25 g (1 oz) dark brown soft sugar
salt and freshly ground black pepper

- Twist each sausage into two smaller pieces and cut apart. Lightly coat a non stick frying pan with cooking spray, add half the sausages and brown for 3–4 minutes, shaking the pan occasionally so that they colour evenly.
- Tip into a flameproof casserole, then brown the remaining sausages in the same way, and add these to the casserole.
- Fry the bacon for 2 minutes in the frying pan, then stir this into the sausages, adding the baked beans, chopped tomatoes, Worcestershire sauce, sugar and seasoning. Bring to a simmer, cover and cook gently for 20 minutes. Serve with medium size baked potatoes (225 g) for an extra 2^1/$_2$ **POINTS** values per serving.

❄
30 POINTS values per recipe
249 calories per serving
Serves 8

Asparagus, parma ham and nectarine salad

Pan-frying the nectarines adds an extra dimension to this salad but, if it's easier, you can just leave them raw. *Takes 15 minutes.*

225 g (8 oz) asparagus tips
150 g (5^1/$_2$ oz) mixed baby salad leaves
6 slices Parma ham, roughly torn
20 g (^{3}/$_4$ oz) Parmesan shavings
low fat cooking spray
6 ripe nectarines, stoned and sliced into wedges
for the dressing
3 tablespoons balsamic vinegar
3 tablespoons clear honey
1^1/$_2$ teaspoons grain mustard
salt and freshly ground black pepper

● Cook the asparagus tips in lightly salted boiling water for 3 minutes or until just tender. Drain and refresh in cold water to stop the cooking process.

● Arrange the salad leaves on a large platter or shallow serving dish and top with the asparagus, Parma ham and Parmesan shavings. Whisk the dressing ingredients together and set aside.

● When ready to serve, lightly coat a non stick frying pan with low fat cooking spray, add the nectarine wedges and fry for about 2 minutes until lightly caramelised; you will need to cook these in two batches. Scatter over the salad, and drizzle on the dressing just before serving.

13^1/$_2$ POINTS values per recipe
124 calories per serving
Serves 6

Citrus-crusted salmon

A whole side of salmon makes for an impressive-looking dish on a buffet, and with a delectable crisp crumb crust, this is positively mouth watering. The salmon can easily be prepared ahead, covered and stored in the fridge until ready to cook. *Takes 8 minutes to prepare, 15 minutes to cook.*

1 x 750 g (1 lb 10 oz) salmon fillet
salt and freshly ground black pepper
4 medium slices bread, torn
4 tablespoons freshly chopped coriander
25 g (1 oz) low fat polyunsaturated margarine,
    melted
zest and juice 1 lemon
zest and juice 1 orange

- Preheat the oven to Gas Mark 5/190°C/fan oven 170°C. Season the salmon and place on a foil-lined baking tray.
- Process the bread and coriander to fine crumbs in a food processor, then mix with the melted margarine, citrus zests and 4 tablespoons of the combined citrus juice. Drizzle the remaining juice over the salmon.
- Press the crumb crust on to the salmon fillet then bake in the oven for 15 minutes until the crust is golden and crisp, and the salmon is cooked through. Transfer to a serving platter and serve hot.

31 POINTS values per recipe
217 calories per serving
Serves 8

Braised pork with apricots

For easy entertaining, this dish can be made ahead then gently reheated before serving. *Takes 25 minutes.*

800 g (1 lb 11 oz) pork fillet, cut into 1 cm ($^1/_2$ inch) slices
salt and freshly ground black pepper
low fat cooking spray
425 ml (15 fl oz) chicken stock
150 ml (5 fl oz) white wine
175 g (6 oz) dried apricots, halved
$^1/_2$ teaspoon mixed spice
1 tablespoon dark soy sauce
4 teaspoons clear honey
2 tablespoons cornflour, mixed with 1 tablespoon cold water
2 tablespoons freshly chopped parsley

● Pat the slices of pork fillet dry on kitchen paper, then season lightly. Coat a non stick frying pan with low fat spray then brown the pork in three batches, cooking for $1^1/_2$ minutes each side.
● As each batch is done, transfer to a flameproof casserole, swirl a little stock around the frying pan to release the flavour and pour into the casserole.
● Place the frying pan back on the heat, coat with a little more low fat cooking spray, then brown the next batch and cook in the same way.
● Pour the white wine into the frying pan and bring to the boil, scraping the bottom of the pan with a spoon to released any caramelised juices.
● Tip into the casserole and stir in the apricots, mixed spice, soy sauce and honey. Bring to a simmer, cover and cook gently for 20 minutes.
● Add the cornflour paste to the casserole, stirring until thickened, then add the parsley and seasoning to taste just before serving.

❄

32 POINTS values per recipe
311 calories per serving
Serves 6

Orange and basil chicken

An excellent dish for serving to a large group of people as it's so quick to prepare and easy to cook. The tangy orange sauce glazes the chicken and keeps it really moist. *Takes 5 minutes to prepare, 20 minutes to cook.*

125 g ($4^1/_2$ oz) marmalade
juice 2 oranges
juice 2 lemons
3 tablespoons freshly chopped basil
salt and freshly ground black pepper
8 x 125 g ($4^1/_2$ oz) skinless boneless chicken breasts

● Preheat the oven to Gas Mark 6/200°C/fan oven 180°C. Blend the marmalade with the citrus juices, basil and seasoning, then pour over the chicken breasts in an ovenproof dish.
● Place the dish in the oven and cook for 20 minutes, basting the chicken with the sauce half way through. Serve on warmed plates.

$21^1/_2$ POINTS values per recipe
176 calories per serving
Serves 8

Rocket, prawn and mango salad

An appetising and colourful salad that looks great as part of a buffet at parties. It's also amazingly low in **POINTS** values and a doddle to prepare.
Takes 15 minutes.

500 g (1 lb 2 oz) cooked and peeled tiger prawns
1 large ripe mango, peeled and sliced
$^3/_4$ cucumber, cut into half moon slices
80 g (3 oz) wild rocket
6 tablespoons sweet chilli sauce
juice 1$^1/_2$ limes
3 tablespoons freshly chopped coriander

● Toss the tiger prawns together with the mango and cucumber slices. Heap the prawn mixture on a large serving plate and scatter the rocket on top.
● Whisk the chilli sauce with the lime juice and coriander and drizzle over the salad just before serving.

$9^1/_2$ **POINTS** values per recipe
128 calories per serving
Serves 6

Marinated olives

Prepare these olives a day ahead if you can, to get the maximum flavour from the marinade. *Takes 10 minutes + marinating.*

400 g (14 oz) mixed whole black and green olives in brine, drained
1 lemon
1 orange
1 teaspoon each coriander and cumin seeds
3 sprigs fresh thyme
2 garlic cloves, sliced
pinch chilli flakes (optional)

● Place the olives on a chopping board and lightly crush with a rolling pin, so that all the flavours of the marinade can penetrate, then place in a bowl.
● Pare four strips of zest from both the lemon and the orange, then squeeze the juice.
● Toast the coriander and cumin seeds in a small pan for 30 seconds or until they smell aromatic.
● Add the citrus zest, juice, thyme, garlic and chilli flakes, if using, and warm through briefly. Pour over the olives, cover and marinate in the fridge for at least 4 hours, but preferably overnight.

Ⓥ *vegan*
8 POINTS values per recipe
48 calories per serving
Serves 8

Smoked salmon and prawn bites

These luxurious little party bites are a doddle to make, but look really impressive. Chill well before slicing, to keep the shape. *Takes 10 minutes + chilling.*

50 g (1³/₄ oz) low fat plain cottage cheese
50 g (1³/₄ oz) low fat soft cheese
75 g (3 oz) cooked and peeled prawns, chopped roughly
1 teaspoon snipped chives
zest ¹/₂ lemon
freshly ground black pepper
4 slices smoked salmon (125 g/4¹/₂ oz)

● Press the cottage cheese through a sieve into a bowl, then blend in the soft cheese. Stir in the prawns, snipped chives, lemon zest and black pepper.
● Lay 2 pieces of cling film out flat on your work surface and place 2 slices of smoked salmon on each, side by side and slightly overlapping. Spoon the prawn mixture down the centre, then use the cling film to help you roll the smoked salmon around the filling, to enclose it.
● Wrap the smoked salmon rolls up tightly in the cling film and twist the ends to secure, then chill in the fridge for at least 30 minutes to firm up. Cut each roll into 6 bites to serve, and arrange on a plate, garnished with chives.

6 POINTS values per recipe
26 calories each
Makes 12 bites

Creamy houmous with vegetable dippers

Perfect for parties, this colourful platter of crudités and houmous also makes a great informal sharing starter with drinks before dinner. *Takes 20 minutes.*

2 x 410 g can chickpeas, drained and rinsed
2 x 150 g cartons 0% fat Greek yogurt
zest and juice 1 lemon
2 garlic cloves, crushed
$1/2$ teaspoon ground cumin plus a pinch to dust
salt and freshly ground black pepper
to serve
250 g (9 oz) cauliflower, broken into small florets
2 red and 2 yellow peppers, deseeded and sliced
125 g ($4^1/2$ oz) mange tout
4 carrots, peeled and cut into batons
285 g (10 oz) cherry tomatoes

• Place the chickpeas in a food processor with the yogurt, lemon zest and juice, garlic and cumin. Whiz to a purée, adding 6–8 tablespoons water as needed to get the right consistency. Season to taste then spoon into a serving bowl and dust with a little extra ground cumin.
• Arrange the vegetable dippers on a platter and serve with the houmous (see photo, page 132).

Ⓥ
11 POINTS values per recipe
143 calories per serving
Serves 8

Marinated prawns in lettuce boats

The simplest summer buffet dish is quick and easy - the prawns just need time to marinate. *Takes 10 minutes + marinating.*

100 g ($3^1/2$ oz) very low fat plain fromage frais
1 small garlic clove, crushed
1 teaspoon grated root ginger
zest and juice $1/2$ lemon
2 tablespoons freshly chopped parsley
2 tablespoons freshly chopped basil
salt and freshly ground black pepper
300 g ($10^1/2$ oz) cooked and peeled tiger prawns
2 Little Gem lettuces

• Stir the fromage frais together with the garlic, ginger, lemon zest and juice, then mix in the herbs and seasoning to taste. Stir the prawns into the mixture and marinate for 10–30 minutes.
• Separate the lettuce leaves and arrange on a serving plate. Spoon a couple of prawns and a little of the marinade on to each lettuce leaf.

$3^1/2$ POINTS values per recipe
24 calories per serving
Makes 12 party bites

Thai infused barbecued tuna

Fresh tuna steaks are ideal to cook on the barbecue as the firm texture holds together well. *Takes 20 minutes to prepare, 5–6 minutes to cook.*

for the tuna
zest 1 lime
1 red chilli, deseeded and diced
1 tablespoon Thai fish sauce
1 tablespoon grated root ginger
$^1/_2$ x 25 g pack fresh coriander, chopped
freshly ground black pepper
6 x 100 g fresh tuna steaks
low fat cooking spray
for the noodle salad
250 g (9 oz) thin rice noodles
2 medium carrots, peeled and grated coarsely
250 g (9 oz) beansprouts, rinsed
juice 1 lime
2 tablespoons Thai fish sauce

- Preheat the barbecue, giving it time to reach a moderate heat. Mix the lime zest, chilli, ginger and coriander with the Thai fish sauce, seasoning with freshly ground black pepper. Rub the mixture into the tuna steaks and leave until ready to barbecue.
- Pour boiling water over the rice noodles in a large bowl and leave to soften for 4 minutes. Drain and rinse in cold water, then mix together with the grated carrot, beansprouts, lime juice and fish sauce.
- When the barbecue has reached the desired cooking heat, lightly spray both the barbecue grill rack and the tuna steaks with low fat cooking spray. Place the tuna steaks on the grill rack and barbecue for 2–3 minutes either side.
Serve with the rice noodle salad, with extra lime wedges to squeeze over the tuna.

22$^1/_2$ POINTS values per recipe
294 calories per serving
Serves 6

Sweet and sour chicken skewers

These colourful skewers should prove a hit with friends and family of all ages. *Takes 25 minutes to prepare + marinating, 15 minutes to cook.*

1 x 432 g can pineapple rings in juice
2 teaspoons Chinese five spice powder
1 large garlic clove, crushed
2 tablespoons soy sauce
4 x 125 g (4$^1/_2$ oz) skinless chicken breast fillets
2 red and 2 yellow peppers, deseeded and quartered

- Drain the juice from the canned pineapple into a non metallic bowl or dish. Stir in the Chinese five spice powder, the garlic and soy sauce.
- Cut each chicken breast into 12 chunky pieces and add to the marinade. Cover and marinate for at least 30 minutes. If using bamboo skewers, soak these in water for 30 minutes to avoid scorching.
- Cut each pineapple ring into eight pieces, then chop each pepper quarter into six chunky pieces. Thread four pieces of each coloured pepper, chicken and pineapple on to each of 12 skewers.
- Cook under a preheated grill for 15 minutes, turning once, until cooked and slightly caramelised. Serve warm or at room temperature.

11 POINTS values per recipe
85 calories per serving
Makes 12 skewers

treat yourself

chapter eight: **something sweet**

Don't worry if you have a sweet tooth, in this chapter you'll find plenty of healthy alternatives that make it possible to enjoy your favourite puddings such as Chocolate pear sponge, Pecan treacle tart and Blueberry baked cheesecake. Switching to lower fat ingredients makes it possible to create dreamy desserts like White chocolate and raspberry cake that are just as satisfyingly sweet as the full fat versions.

White chocolate and raspberry cake

This rich layered cake is perfect for a special occasion. *Takes 20 minutes to prepare, 20 minutes to cook.*

low fat cooking spray

for the sponge

100 g (3¹/₂ oz) low fat polyunsaturated margarine

100 g (3¹/₂ oz) caster sugar

175 g (6 oz) self raising flour, sifted

2 medium eggs

¹/₂ teaspoon vanilla extract

4 tablespoons skimmed milk

pinch of salt

for the filling

50 g (1³/₄ oz) white cooking chocolate

150 g (5¹/₂ oz) low fat soft cheese

2 tablespoons icing sugar

200 g (7 oz) raspberries

- Preheat the oven to Gas Mark 3/160°C/fan oven 140°C. Lightly grease two 18 cm (7 inch) cake tins with low fat cooking spray and line them with baking parchment.
- Place all the sponge ingredients together in a mixing bowl and beat for 2–3 minutes, using an electric whisk, until pale and fluffy. Divide between the prepared cake tins and spread out evenly. Bake for 18–20 minutes until risen and springy to the touch. Turn out on to a wire rack to cool.
- Use a vegetable peeler to make 10 g (¹/₄ oz) white chocolate shavings to top the cake, and set aside in the fridge.
- Break up the remaining chocolate and place in a heatproof bowl set over a pan of gently simmering water until melted. Cool slightly, then beat in the soft cheese and icing sugar until smooth. Chill in the fridge until needed.
- To make up the cake, spread half the white chocolate frosting over one layer of sponge and

gently press in the raspberries. Top with the second sponge and spread the remaining frosting on top. Scatter the white chocolate shavings over the cake. Keep in the fridge until ready to serve.

✳ *unfilled sponge* Ⓥ
37¹/₂ POINTS values per recipe
211 calories per serving
Serves 10

Apple and almond crumble

Serve this traditional apple crumble with either a scoop of low fat vanilla ice cream for a **POINTS** value of 1 or a 150 g pot of low fat custard for a **POINTS** value of 2. *Takes 15 minutes to prepare, 20–25 minutes to cook.*

600 g (1 lb 5 oz) Bramley cooking apples, peeled, cored and sliced
1 eating apple, peeled, cored and sliced
60 g (2 oz) soft light brown sugar
1 teaspoon ground cinnamon
50 g (1³/₄ oz) low fat polyunsaturated margarine
100 g (3¹/₂ oz) plain flour, sifted
40 g (1¹/₂ oz) porridge oats
15 g (¹/₂ oz) flaked almonds

● Preheat the oven to Gas Mark 4/180°C/160°C fan oven.
● Place the apples in a medium saucepan with 20 g (³/₄ oz) sugar, ¹/₂ teaspoon cinnamon and 125 ml (4 fl oz) water. Cover and cook over a medium heat for 7–8 minutes, until the apples start to soften then tip into a 20 cm (8 inch) baking dish.
● Meanwhile, rub the margarine into the flour until crumbly, then stir in the rest of the sugar, cinnamon, oats and almonds. Press the crumble topping down on to the fruit, then bake in the centre of the oven for 20–25 minutes, until the crumble is golden brown, crisp and bubbling.

Ⓥ
22 POINTS values per recipe
210 calories per serving
Serves 6

Strawberry and hazelnut strata

The toasted hazelnut and crumb mixture adds a tasty crunch factor to this layered dessert.
Takes 10 minutes to prepare, 8 minutes to cook.

40 g (1¹/₂ oz) fresh breadcrumbs
25 g (1 oz) demerara sugar
15 g (¹/₂ oz) chopped hazelnuts
300 g (10¹/₂ oz) strawberries, sliced
1 tablespoon icing sugar
500 g carton low fat custard, chilled

● Preheat the oven to Gas Mark 4/180°C/fan oven 160°C.
● Mix the breadcrumbs with the sugar and hazelnuts and spread out on a tray lined with baking parchment.
● Bake for 8 minutes, stirring halfway through, until the crumbs are caramelised and crisp. Cool.
● Mix the strawberries with the icing sugar to sweeten.
● Layer the chilled custard, strawberries and crunchy hazelnut crumbs into four dessert glasses or bowls. Serve immediately.

Ⓥ
13 POINTS values per recipe
206 calories per serving
Serves 4

Jammy bread and butter pudding

A fun twist on classic bread and butter pudding, this is a recipe that will certainly be popular with the whole family. *Takes 10 minutes to prepare, 30 minutes to cook.*

8 medium slices white bread
8 heaped teaspoons raspberry jam
15 g (^{1}/$_2$ oz) low fat polyunsaturated margarine
100 g (3^1/$_2$ oz) raspberries
low fat cooking spray
4 medium eggs, beaten
60 g (2 oz) caster sugar
400 ml (14 fl oz) skimmed milk

● Preheat the oven to Gas Mark 4/180°C/fan oven 160°C.
● Make four rounds of jam sandwiches with the bread and jam, then spread the margarine over the top of each sandwich.
● Cut each one into four triangles, and place in a baking dish, lightly greased with low fat cooking spray, that holds the sandwiches snugly. Scatter the raspberries in and amongst the sandwiches.
● Beat the eggs together with the sugar and milk, then pour into the dish, making sure that the bread is evenly covered.
● Cover with a sheet of foil, lightly greased with low fat cooking spray, then bake for 20 minutes. Remove the foil and cook for a further 10 minutes until golden brown and crisp on top.

Ⓥ
26 POINTS values per recipe
245 calories per serving
Serves 6

Pear and ginger tarte tatin

Look out for all butter puff pastry, which has a fantastic flavour and lightness, without adding extra **POINTS** values. *Takes 10 minutes to prepare, 20 minutes to cook.*

2 pieces stem ginger in syrup, chopped finely, plus 2 tablespoons syrup from the jar
2 x 210 g cans pear halves in juice, drained
1 teaspoon plain flour
125 g (4^1/$_2$ oz) puff pastry

● Preheat the oven to Gas Mark 6/200°C/ fan oven 180°C.
● Place the chopped stem ginger and syrup in the base of a 24 cm (9^1/$_2$ inch) metal pie plate, then arrange the pear halves to fit in snugly, rounded side down.
● Dust the work surface with the flour and roll out the pastry to fit neatly inside the pie dish. Lift on top and tuck the pastry around the fruit at the edges.
● Place on a baking tray and cook for 20 minutes or until the pastry is well risen and crisp. Turn out on to a plate to serve.

Ⓥ
18 POINTS values per recipe
126 calories per serving
Serves 6

Chocolate pear sponge

A light chocolate sponge pudding, drizzled with hot chocolate sauce – scrumptious. *Takes 10 minutes to prepare, 30 minutes to cook.*

low fat cooking spray

410 g can pear halves in juice, drained

200 g (7 oz) self raising flour

salt

2 tablespoons cocoa powder

150 g (5^1/$_2$ oz) caster sugar

100 g (3^1/$_2$ oz) low fat polyunsaturated margarine

2 medium eggs

100 g (3^1/$_2$ oz) low fat plain yogurt

for the sauce

2 tablespoons cornflour

1 tablespoon cocoa powder

1 tablespoon caster sugar

300 ml (10 fl oz) skimmed milk

● Preheat the oven to Gas Mark 4/180°C/ fan oven 160°C. Lightly grease a 23 cm (9 inch) diameter ceramic baking dish with low fat cooking spray. Pat the pears dry on kitchen paper and place in the dish, cut side down.

● Sift the flour, salt and cocoa into a mixing bowl. Add the sugar, margarine, eggs and yogurt and beat for 2 minutes using an electric whisk. Add a little water, if needed, to give a mixture that drops easily from a spoon, then spread over the pears.

● Bake for 30 minutes, or until the sponge is well risen and firm to the touch.

● For the sauce, mix the cornflour, cocoa and sugar together in a non stick saucepan. Add a little of the milk to mix to a paste, then gradually blend in the remainder. Bring to the boil, stirring continuously, and simmer for 2 minutes.

● Run a knife around the edge of the baking dish and turn the pudding out on to a large plate. Cut into slices and serve with the hot chocolate sauce.

Ⓥ

39^1/$_2$ POINTS values per recipe

301 calories per serving

Serves 8

Christmas pudding with brandy sauce

15 minutes to prepare + soaking, $2^{1}/_{2}$ hours to cook.

150 g ($5^{1}/_{2}$ oz) mixed dried fruit
zest and juice 1 orange
2 tablespoons brandy (optional)
low fat cooking spray
100 g ($3^{1}/_{2}$ oz) low fat polyunsaturated margarine
100 g ($3^{1}/_{2}$ oz) soft dark brown sugar
100 g ($3^{1}/_{2}$ oz) fresh breadcrumbs
2 medium eggs, beaten
2 teaspoons mixed spice
150 g ($5^{1}/_{2}$ oz) carrot, peeled and coarsely grated
$^{1}/_{2}$ teaspoon bicarbonate of soda

for the sauce
40 g ($1^{1}/_{2}$ oz) cornflour
50 g ($1^{3}/_{4}$ oz) soft light brown sugar
600 ml (1 pint) skimmed milk
2 tablespoons brandy

● Mix the dried fruit with the orange zest, juice and brandy (if using). Cover, and leave to soak for at least 4 hours. Lightly grease a 1.2 litre (2 pint) pudding basin with low fat cooking spray.
● Cream the margarine and sugar together until fluffy. Add the breadcrumbs, eggs, mixed spice, soaked fruits and carrot. Stir in the bicarb, blended with a little warm water. Spoon the mixture into the basin, cover with a sheet of baking parchment and a sheet of foil and secure under the rim with string. Place in a large saucepan and pour in boiling water to a third of the way up the basin. Cover and simmer for $2^{1}/_{2}$ hours. Add more water if necessary.
● For the sauce, mix the cornflour and sugar in a non stick pan; gradually stir in the milk. Bring to the boil, stirring, until smooth and thick. Simmer for 3 minutes, add the brandy, and pour into a jug.

❄ Ⓨ
35 POINTS values per recipe
280 calories per serving
Serves 8

Pecan treacle tart

A low **POINTS** value version of this lusciously sweet and sticky pudding. Serve warm, with a scoop of low fat vanilla ice cream for an extra 1 **POINTS** value. *Takes 20 minutes to prepare + chilling, 25 minutes to cook.*

100 g ($3^{1}/_{2}$ oz) plain flour, plus 1 teaspoon for rolling
50 g ($1^{3}/_{4}$ oz) low fat polyunsaturated margarine
200 g (7 oz) golden syrup
zest and juice $^{1}/_{2}$ lemon
40 g ($1^{1}/_{2}$ oz) fresh breadcrumbs
25 g (1 oz) pecans, chopped
1 medium egg, beaten

● Sift the flour into a bowl and rub in the margarine until the mixture is crumbly. Mix in just enough cold water to bring the pastry together in a ball. Flatten into a disc, wrap in cling film, and chill for 30 minutes.
● Preheat the oven to Gas Mark 5/190°C/fan oven 170°C.
● Warm the golden syrup with the lemon zest and juice until just runny. Stir in the breadcrumbs and leave to swell for 5 minutes.
● Dust the work surface with 1 teaspoon flour and roll out the pastry to fit a 24 cm ($9^{1}/_{2}$ inch) metal pie plate (or a disposable foil pie plate if you don't have one).
● Mix the pecans and beaten egg into the syrupy breadcrumbs, then pour the filling into the pastry case, place on a baking tray and bake for 25 minutes until the filling is set. Let the tart cool for at least 15 minutes before eating, as the filling will be very hot.

Ⓨ
$23^{1}/_{2}$ POINTS values per recipe
250 calories per serving
Serves 6

Fruity rice sundae

A mixture of fruits layered with sweet, creamy rice.
Takes 25–30 minutes + cooling.

110 g (4 oz) pudding rice or risotto rice
850 ml (1^1/$_2$ pints) skimmed milk
1^1/$_2$ teaspoons vanilla extract
3 tablespoons granulated artificial sweetener
410 g can apricot halves in juice, drained
2 medium bananas, sliced
150 g (5^1/$_2$ oz) raspberries

- Place the rice and milk in a non stick pan, bring to the boil, stirring, then simmer gently for 25–30 minutes until the rice is tender and thickened.
- Transfer to a bowl, stir in the vanilla and sweetener and press cling film on to the surface to prevent a skin from forming. Leave to cool.
- To serve, divide the apricots between four dishes or glasses, add half the cooled rice, then a layer of banana, followed by the rest of the rice.
- Top with the raspberries and serve.

Ⓥ
13^1/$_2$ POINTS values per recipe
268 calories per serving
Serves 4

Blueberry baked cheesecake

Baked cheesecakes tend to crack if they cool too quickly, so to avoid this leave the cooked cheesecake in the turned off oven to cool. *Takes 15 minutes to prepare, 35 minutes to cook + cooling.*

6 large caramel rice cakes
2 ripe medium bananas, mashed
500 g (1 lb 2 oz) Quark
200 g (7 oz) very low fat plain fromage frais
3 medium eggs
2 teaspoons vanilla extract
3 tablespoons granulated artificial sweetener
150 g (5¹/₂ oz) fresh blueberries

- Preheat the oven to Gas Mark 4/180°C/ fan oven 160°C.
- Process the rice cakes to rough crumbs in a food processor, then mix into the mashed bananas.
- Press into the base of a 20 cm (8 inch) springform cake tin, then bake in the oven for 10 minutes until firm.
- Remove from the oven and reduce the temperature to Gas Mark 2/150°C/fan oven 130°C.
- Wipe out the processor bowl then whiz together the Quark, fromage frais, eggs, vanilla and sweetener until smooth.
- Pour half of the mixture over the cheesecake base and scatter with half the blueberries. Add the remaining cheesecake mixture and blueberries, and shake gently to level the surface.
- Bake in the oven for 35 minutes, until the cheesecake is set in the centre, but still slightly wobbly. Turn off the oven, but leave the cheesecake in as it cools.
- Chill before serving, then carefully unmould and cut into slices.

Ⓥ
19 POINTS values per recipe
181 calories per serving
Serves 10

Peach Melba

Peach Melba was a dish created in honour of the opera singer, Dame Nellie Melba, and is a classic summery combination of peaches and raspberries. Using tinned peaches and frozen raspberries means that you can enjoy this dessert all year round. *Takes 10 minutes.*

200 g (7 oz) fresh or frozen raspberries, defrosted
1 tablespoon + 2 teaspoons artificial granulated
    sweetener
175 g (6 oz) low fat soft cheese
few drops almond extract
2 x 411 g cans peach halves in juice, drained

● Whiz the raspberries to a puree with 1 tablespoon sweetener in a liquidiser, or using a hand held blender. Press through a sieve to remove the seeds.
● Mix the low fat soft cheese with 2 teaspoons sweetener and a couple of drops of almond extract, then spoon the mixture into the peach halves.
● Serve with the raspberry sauce poured over the peaches.

Ⓥ
8 POINTS values per recipe
122 calories per serving
Serves 4

Raspberry and passion fruit meringues

Exotic flavoured passion fruit seeds and raspberries set off the sweetness of these **Core Plan** meringues. Serve the meringues on the day of baking, to retain their crisp texture. *Takes 5 minutes to prepare, 1 hour to cook.*

4 medium egg whites
6 level tablespoons granulated artificial sweetener
2 x 150 g cartons 0% fat Greek yogurt
150 g (5$^{1}/_{2}$ oz) raspberries
2 passion fruits, halved

● Preheat the oven to Gas Mark $^{1}/_{2}$ /120°C/fan oven 100°C. Line a baking tray with non stick baking parchment.
● Using an electric whisk, beat the egg whites to stiff peaks, then whisk in the sweetener.
● Spoon four mounds on to the prepared tray, then use a dampened spoon to shape them into rounds and hollow out the centre to make meringue nests.
● Bake in the oven for 1 hour, then cool.
● To serve, spoon the yogurt into the centre of each meringue, top with raspberries and the seeds of half a passion fruit. Serve immediately.

Ⓥ
3 POINTS values per recipe
85 calories per serving
Serves 4

Lemon and lime cheesecake pots

These tangy little cheesecake pots feel like a real indulgence. *Takes 8 minutes + chilling and cooling.*

12 g sachet lemon and lime sugar free jelly
juice ¹/₂ lemon
juice ¹/₂ lime
150 g (5¹/₂ oz) low fat natural yogurt
100 g (3¹/₂ oz) low fat soft cheese
100 g (3¹/₂ oz) grapes, halved

● Sprinkle the jelly crystals over 250 ml (9 fl oz) boiling water and stir to dissolve. Add the lemon and lime juice, then leave to cool to body temperature, stirring occasionally (this will take about 15 minutes).
● Mix the yogurt into the low fat soft cheese in a mixing bowl, stirring briskly until smooth. Gradually whisk the cooled jelly into the cheesecake mixture, until evenly blended. Pour into 4 ramekins, cover and chill for around 2 hours or until set.
● Uncover the cheesecake pots and serve topped with the halved grapes.

5 POINTS values per recipe
71 calories per serving
Serves 4

Vanilla mousses with plums

These vanilla flavoured mousses are like panna cotta, but with far fewer **POINTS** values. *Takes 15 minutes to prepare + chilling, 20–25 minutes to cook.*

350 ml (12 fl oz) skimmed milk
12 g sachet powdered gelatine
1 vanilla pod or 1 teaspoon vanilla extract
2 tablespoons granulated artificial sweetener
300 g (10¹/₂ oz) low fat plain yogurt
for the plums
6 plums, halved and stoned
juice 1 large orange
1 teaspoon granulated artificial sweetener

● Measure 4 tablespoons of milk into a small bowl, sprinkle on the gelatine and leave to swell for 5 minutes.
● Cut the vanilla pod in half, if using, and scrape the seeds into the remaining milk in a saucepan. Add the pod. Gently bring the milk to a simmer.
● Add the soaked gelatine and stir until dissolved. Remove from the heat and stir in the sweetener.
● Pour into a large mixing bowl and leave to cool for 5 minutes. If using the vanilla pod, remove at this point, but if not, stir in the vanilla extract.
● Mix the yogurt into the cooled milk. Pour the mixture into four mini pudding basins or ramekins. Cover and refrigerate for 2–3 hours until set.
● For the roasted plums, preheat the oven to Gas Mark 5/190°C/fan oven 170°C. Place the halved plums in an ovenproof dish, cut side up, pour in the orange juice and sprinkle with sweetener.
● Roast in the oven for 20–25 minutes, depending on ripeness, until the plums are tender and slightly caramelised. Baste with the juices a couple of times during cooking. Serve the plums warm or cooled, with the turned out yogurt mousses.

7 POINTS values per recipe
137 calories per serving
Serves 4

Spiced glazed pineapple

A fabulously fast fruity pud based on storecupboard ingredients. *Takes 5 minutes.*

220 g can pineapple slices in juice
pinch cinnamon
freshly grated nutmeg
1 teaspoon granulated artificial sweetener
zest of ¹/₂ lime

● Drain the pineapple juice into a jug and mix with the cinnamon, a few gratings of nutmeg and the sweetener. Set aside.

● Pat the pineapple dry on kitchen paper and preheat a non stick frying pan on the hob. Add the pineapple rings and fry for 1¹/₂–2 minutes each side until caramelised. Pour in the spiced juice and bubble for 15–20 seconds until slightly syrupy.

● Spoon the pineapple and sauce on to two plates and top with the grated lime zest. Serve immediately.

Ⓥ *vegan*
1¹/₂ POINTS values per recipe
57 calories per serving
Serves 2

Blackcurrant mousse

This recipe turns a sachet of sugar free jelly into a stunning but easy, dessert. *Takes 20 minutes to prepare + chilling.*

12 g sachet blackcurrant sugar free jelly
juice ¹/₂ lemon
290 g can blackcurrants in juice
2 egg whites
150 g (5¹/₂ oz) low fat plain yogurt

● Sprinkle the sugar free jelly crystals into 200 ml (7 fl oz) boiling water, stirring to dissolve.

● Add the lemon juice and the juice from the can of blackcurrants. If necessary, add cold water to make the jelly up to 400 ml (14 fl oz). Pour into a large bowl and chill in the fridge for 30 minutes until starting to thicken.

● Whisk the egg whites to the soft peak stage. Stir the yogurt into the thickening jelly, then fold in the egg whites.

● Ladle into four ramekins, cover and chill for 3 hours or until set. To serve, spoon the blackcurrants on top of each mousse.

Ⓥ
2¹/₂ POINTS values per recipe
61 calories per serving
Serves 4

chapter nine: **cakes and bakes**

You just can't beat the fabulous aroma and flavour of a slice of homemade Peach crumble cake or a Cranberry and almond cookie warm from the oven. Baking is so therapeutic and the recipes in this chapter are much better for you than store-bought versions which are often packed with sweeteners, additives and preservatives, as well as unhealthy forms of fats. And of course they taste so much better too. Take your pick of these recipes from Cherry scones and Chocolate mocha fudge cake to a festive Fruity tea loaf.

warm from the oven

Banana and apricot loaf cake

A light, fruity loaf cake that keeps well for a couple of days. The topping of crunchy seeds adds texture. *Takes 15 minutes to prepare, 50–60 minutes to cook.*

low fat cooking spray
2 ripe medium bananas, mashed
2 medium eggs, separated
150 g (5^1/$_2$ oz) low fat plain yogurt
80 g (3 oz) soft light brown sugar
100 g (3^1/$_2$ oz) dried apricots, chopped
250 g (9 oz) self raising flour
salt
1 tablespoon pumpkin or sunflower seeds

- Preheat the oven to Gas Mark 4/180°C/fan oven 160°C. Lightly grease a 900 g (2 lb) loaf tin with low fat cooking spray and line it with baking parchment.
- Mix the mashed bananas with the egg yolks, yogurt, sugar and apricots.
- Sift in the flour and a pinch of salt, then stir together until well mixed. In a separate bowl, whisk the egg whites to soft peaks.
- Stir a spoonful into the cake batter to slacken the mixture, then carefully fold in the remainder. Pour into the loaf tin and scatter the seeds on top.
- Bake on the centre shelf of the oven for 50–60 minutes, or until a skewer comes out clean.
- Cool in the tin for 10 minutes before turning out on to a wire rack to cool completely.

❄ Ⓥ
27^1/$_2$ POINTS values per recipe
155 calories per serving
Serves 12

Peach crumble cake

Ideal with a cup of coffee, this cake can also be served warm as a pudding with a 150 g low fat custard, for an extra 2 **POINTS** values. *Takes 10 minutes to prepare, 50 minutes to cook.*

low fat cooking spray
275 g (9^1/$_2$ oz) self raising flour
1 teaspoon cinnamon
salt
125 g (4^1/$_2$ oz) low fat polyunsaturated margarine
125 g (4^1/$_2$ oz) soft light brown sugar
3 medium eggs, beaten
200 g (7 oz) low fat plain yogurt
410 g can peach slices in juice, drained

- Preheat the oven to Gas Mark 4/180°C/ fan oven 160°C. Grease a 20 cm (8 inch) springform cake tin with low fat cooking spray and line it with baking parchment.
- Sift the flour, cinnamon and a pinch of salt into a mixing bowl. Rub in the margarine until the mixture is crumbly, then stir in the sugar. Weigh out 80 g (3 oz) of the mixture into a small bowl for the topping and set this aside.
- Mix the eggs and yogurt into the remaining flour mixture to form a smooth batter, then pour into the prepared cake tin.
- Pat the peaches dry on kitchen paper, then arrange on top of the cake.
- Scatter with the reserved crumb mixture, then bake the cake in the oven for 45–50 minutes, or until a skewer inserted in the centre comes out clean. Cool on a wire rack. The cake can be stored for 2–3 days.

❄ Ⓥ
39 POINTS values per recipe
196 calories per serving
Serves 12

Cinnamon prune buns

These sweet and sticky rolls are based on Chelsea buns, with a filling of moist prunes and cinnamon sugar. *Takes 25 minutes to prepare + 30 minutes to prove, 20–25 minutes to cook.*

350 g (12 oz) plain flour, plus 1 tablespoon for
    kneading and rolling
$^1/_2$ teaspoon salt
7 g sachet active dried yeast
30 g (1$^1/_4$ oz) low fat polyunsaturated margarine
1 medium egg, beaten
150 ml (5 fl oz) skimmed milk, warmed to body
    temperature
2 teaspoons cinnamon
40 g (1$^1/_2$ oz) soft light brown sugar
200 g (7 oz) dried prunes, chopped
low fat cooking spray
1 tablespoon clear honey, warmed

● Sift the flour and salt into a mixing bowl, stir in the yeast, then rub in half the margarine.
● Make a well in the centre, then mix in the egg and enough warmed milk to make a soft, but not sticky, dough that comes away from the bowl.
● Dust the work surface with $^1/_2$ tablespoon flour, turn the dough out and knead for 3–4 minutes until soft and springy.
● Return the dough to the bowl, cover with cling film and leave to rise in a warm place for 1$^1/_2$ hours or until doubled in size.
● Sprinkle the remaining flour on to the work surface and roll out the dough to a 25 x 35 cm (10 x 14 inch) rectangle.
● Melt the remaining margarine and brush all over the dough.
● Mix the cinnamon and sugar together and sprinkle on evenly. Scatter the prunes on top and press in lightly.
● Starting from one of the long sides roll up the dough tightly, then slice into 12 pieces. Transfer to a roasting tin, lightly greased with low fat cooking spray, that will hold the buns fairly snugly, cover with cling film and leave to prove and swell for 30 minutes.
● Preheat the oven to Gas Mark 4/180°C/ fan oven 160°C.
● Bake the buns for 20–25 minutes until puffy, golden and springy. Remove from the oven and brush with the warmed honey. Serve slightly warm.

❋ Ⓥ
30 POINTS values per recipe
168 calories per serving
Makes 12

2½
POINTS
VALUE®

Fruity tea loaf

A luscious combination of dried fruits make this fatless tea loaf really moist and tasty. *Takes 10 minutes to prepare + soaking, 50–60 minutes to cook.*

1 tea bag
100 g (3$^1/_2$ oz) dried prunes, chopped
100 g (3$^1/_2$ oz) dried apricots, chopped
100 g (3$^1/_2$ oz) sultanas
low fat cooking spray
225 g (8 oz) self raising flour
2 teaspoons mixed spice
salt
150 g (5$^1/_2$ oz) demerara sugar
1 medium egg, beaten
3 tablespoons skimmed milk

- Make 250 ml (9 fl oz) tea with the tea bag and boiling water. Mix the dried fruits together in a bowl, pour on the hot tea, cover, and leave to soak for 4–5 hours, or overnight.
- Preheat the oven to Gas Mark 4/180°C/ fan oven 160°C. Grease a 900 g (2 lb) loaf tin with low fat cooking spray and line with baking parchment.
- Sift the flour, mixed spice and a pinch of salt into a mixing bowl, then stir in all but 1 tablespoon of the sugar.
- Mix the soaked fruits (and any liquid that has not been absorbed), egg and milk into the flour to form a batter. Pour into the loaf tin and scatter with the reserved sugar.
- Bake in the oven on the centre shelf for 50–60 minutes, or until a skewer inserted in the centre comes out clean.
- Cool on a wire rack, then store in an airtight container for up to a week.

❄ Ⓥ
30 POINTS values per recipe
162 calories per serving
Serves 12

Carrot and pineapple squares

Tempting squares of luscious frosted carrot and pineapple cake. Individual pieces can be wrapped in cling film and frozen if you wish. *Takes 20 minutes to prepare, 25–30 minutes to cook.*

low fat cooking spray
3 medium eggs
100 g (3¹/₂ oz) caster sugar
80 g (3 oz) low fat polyunsaturated margarine, melted
200 g (7 oz) self raising flour
2 teaspoons mixed spice
salt
250 g (9 oz) carrots, peeled and grated coarsely
432 g can crushed pineapple, well drained
for the frosting
100 g (3¹/₂ oz) low fat soft cheese
60 g (2 oz) very low fat plain fromage frais
1 tablespoon icing sugar, sifted
¹/₄ teaspoon mixed spice

• Preheat the oven to Gas Mark 4/180°C/ fan oven 160°C.

• Lightly grease an 18 x 28 cm (7 x 11 inch) rectangular baking tin with low fat cooking spray and line it with baking parchment .

• Beat the eggs and sugar with an electric whisk until creamy and thick. Pour in the melted margarine, then sift in the flour, 2 teaspoons mixed spice and a pinch of salt.

• Fold in to give a smooth batter, then stir in the grated carrots and drained pineapple.

• Spoon into the prepared tin and then smooth the top. Bake on the centre shelf of the oven for 25–30 minutes until the cake is risen and firm to the touch. Turn out and cool on a wire rack.

• To make the frosting, beat the soft cheese with the fromage frais and icing sugar until smooth. Spread evenly over the cooled cake and dust with the mixed spice.

• Cut into squares, and store in an airtight container in the fridge for up to 3 days.

❄ Ⓥ
33 POINTS values per recipe
135 calories per serving
Makes 15

Chocolate mocha fudge cake

An indulgent cake or dessert with an intense flavour. Measure out all the ingredients before you start whisking, so that you don't lose the air that gives this cake its lightness. *Takes 25 minutes to prepare, 20 minutes to cook.*

low fat cooking spray

175 g (6 oz) soft light brown sugar

2 medium eggs, plus 3 egg whites

100 g ($3^1/_2$ oz) self raising flour

15 g ($^1/_2$ oz) cocoa powder

$^1/_2$ teaspoon baking powder

salt

100 g ($3^1/_2$ oz) instant dry polenta or cornmeal

275 g ($9^1/_2$ oz) low fat plain yogurt

1 teaspoon vanilla extract

25 g (1 oz) luxury dark chocolate (minimum 70% cocoa solids), grated

2 tablespoons instant coffee

2 tablespoons icing sugar

for the frosting

3 tablespoons icing sugar

2 tablespoons cocoa powder

1 teaspoon instant coffee

150 g ($5^1/_2$ oz) low fat soft cheese

● Preheat the oven to Gas Mark 4/180°C/ fan oven 160°C. Grease two 18 cm (7 inch) cake tins with low fat cooking spray and line them with baking parchment.

● Beat the sugar with the whole eggs for 2–3 minutes, using an electric whisk, until pale and thick. Sift the flour, cocoa, baking powder and a pinch of salt over the egg mixture and beat in until smooth.

● Stir in the polenta, yogurt, vanilla and half the grated chocolate (reserve the rest for the topping).

● Clean the beaters thoroughly, then, in a separate bowl, beat the egg whites to the soft peak stage.

● Stir a spoonful of beaten egg whites into the cake batter to loosen the mixture, then carefully fold in the remainder. Pour into the cake tins and level the surface.

● Bake the sponges on the centre shelf for 20 minutes or until risen and firm.

● Dissolve the coffee and icing sugar in 4 tablespoons boiling water and drizzle this evenly over the sponges.

● Cool in the tins for 10 minutes, then carefully remove from the tins and peel off the lining paper. Cool on a wire rack.

● To make the frosting, sift the icing sugar and cocoa powder into a bowl. Stir in the instant coffee and beat together with the low fat soft cheese until smooth. Spread the frosting over both layers of cake, then stack one on top of the other. Sprinkle with the reserved grated chocolate.

❄ Ⓥ

37 POINTS values per recipe

202 calories per serving

Serves 12

Cherry scones

These scones have a superbly light texture and are irresistible with a cup of tea. *Takes 15 minutes to prepare, 15 minutes to cook.*

1 tablespoon lemon juice
150 ml (5 fl oz) skimmed milk
225 g (8 oz) self raising flour
$^1/_2$ teaspoon cream of tartar
salt
40 g (1$^1/_2$ oz) low fat polyunsaturated margarine
25 g (1 oz) caster sugar
60 g (2 oz) glacé cherries, chopped
low fat cooking spray

- Preheat the oven to Gas Mark 6/200°C/ fan oven 180°C.
- Mix the lemon juice with the milk and set aside to thicken and curdle. Set aside 1 teaspoon flour for rolling out, then sift the remaining flour, cream of tartar and a pinch of salt into a bowl.
- Rub in the margarine until the mixture looks like crumbs, then stir in the sugar and cherries. Make a well in the centre.
- Reserve 2 tablespoons of the milk to brush the tops of the scones, then mix enough of the remaining milk into the flour mixture to give a soft but not sticky dough.
- Dust the work surface with the reserved flour and roll out the dough to 2 cm ($^3/_4$ inch) deep.
- Cut out 12 x 5 cm (2 inch) scones using a cutter, re-rolling the scone dough as needed.
- Place on a baking tray, lightly greased with low fat cooking spray, then brush the tops with the reserved milk. Bake for 12–15 minutes until well risen and golden brown. Cool slightly on a wire rack before eating.

❄ Ⓥ
19 POINTS values per recipe
100 calories per serving
Makes 12

Cranberry and almond cookies

These little cookies are soft and chewy when still warm, then they crisp up as they cool. Store in an airtight container. *Takes 10 minutes to prepare, 10 minutes to cook.*

100 g (3$^1/_2$ oz) clear honey
50 g (1$^3/_4$ oz) low fat polyunsaturated margarine
60 g (2 oz) dried cranberries
15 g ($^1/_2$ oz) flaked almonds
80 g (3 oz) porridge oats
80 g (3 oz) self raising flour

- Preheat the oven to Gas Mark 4/180°C/fan oven 160°C.
- Measure the honey and margarine into a small pan and heat gently until melted.
- Mix the cranberries, almonds, porridge oats and flour together in a bowl, then pour in the honey mixture. Stir to bring together.
- Spoon on to a baking try lightly greased with low fat cooking spray, in 16 mounds. Flatten slightly with the back of a spoon.
- Bake for 10 minutes until set and golden brown, then cool on a wire rack.

Ⓥ
21 POINTS values per recipe
84 calories per serving
Makes 16

Banana oat bars

These spongy banana oat bars are packed with energy-giving ingredients. Grab one for breakfast on the run. *Takes 15 minutes to prepare, 30 minutes to cook.*

low fat cooking spray
100 g (3¹/₂ oz) porridge oats
2 tablespoons granulated artificial sweetener
¹/₂ teaspoon cream of tartar
¹/₂ teaspoon ground cinnamon
3 ripe medium bananas, mashed
2 medium eggs, separated
150 g (5¹/₂ oz) low fat plain yogurt

- Preheat the oven to Gas Mark 4/180°C/ fan oven 160°C. Lightly grease a 20 cm (8 inch) square cake tin with low fat cooking spray and line it with baking parchment.
- Reserve 1 tablespoon oats to top the bars, then whiz the rest to a powder in a food processor.
- Mix with the sweetener, cream of tartar and cinnamon, then add the mashed bananas, egg yolks and yogurt.
- In a separate bowl, whisk the egg whites to soft peaks. Stir a spoonful into the banana oat batter to loosen it, then carefully fold in the remainder.
- Pour into the prepared tin and scatter with the reserved oats.
- Bake on the centre shelf of the oven for 30 minutes until firm and springy. Cool in the tin, set on a wire rack.
- Cut into ten fingers and store in an airtight container, or wrap individual bars in cling film and freeze.

❄ Ⓥ
14 POINTS values per recipe
99 calories per serving
Makes 10

Festive
fruit cake

A jewel-like, glazed fruit topping makes a change from the usual marzipan and icing covering on this traditional rich fruit cake. Ideally, store the cake for at least 2 weeks before decorating and eating, to allow the flavour to develop. It can be stored for up to 3 months. *Takes 30 minutes to prepare + soaking, 2^1/$_2$ hours to cook + 15 minutes to decorate.*

zest and juice 1 orange

zest and juice 1 lemon

2 tablespoons brandy, rum or whisky (optional)

150 g (5^1/$_2$ oz) dried prunes, chopped

50 g (1^3/$_4$ oz) glacé cherries, chopped

350 g (12 oz) mixed dried fruit

1 tablespoon ground mixed spice

low fat cooking spray

100 g (3^1/$_2$ oz) low fat polyunsaturated margarine

100 g (3^1/$_2$ oz) soft dark brown sugar

4 medium eggs

200 g (7 oz) plain flour, sifted

1 medium Bramley apple, peeled and grated coarsely

40 g (1^1/$_2$ oz) blanched almonds, chopped roughly

to decorate

100 g (3^1/$_2$ oz) apricot jam

1 tablespoon lemon juice

100 g (3^1/$_2$ oz) dried prunes

150 g (5^1/$_2$ oz) dried apricots

40 g (1^1/$_2$ oz) glacé cherries

● Mix the first seven ingredients together and leave to soak for at least 2 hours, or overnight if you can.

● Preheat the oven to Gas Mark 2/150°C/ fan oven 130°C. Grease with low fat cooking spray and line a 20 cm (8 inch) round deep cake tin.

● Cream the margarine and sugar together until light and fluffy, then beat in the eggs one at a time, adding a spoonful of flour with each egg.

● Stir in the remaining flour, the apple, almonds and soaked fruits and mix well.

● Pour into the cake tin, cover with a sheet of baking parchment, and bake on the centre shelf for 2^1/$_4$–2^1/$_2$ hours. To test whether the cake is done, insert a skewer into the centre and leave for a few seconds. It should come out looking clean and dry; if it is covered in sticky cake mixture then the cake needs to be cooked a little longer.

● Cool the cake in the tin for 15 minutes before turning out, then cool completely on a wire rack. Wrap the cake in baking parchment and foil to store.

● To decorate, gently heat the apricot jam and lemon juice in a small pan, then let it cool for 10 minutes.

● Brush the top of the cake with a little jam to make it sticky, then arrange the dried fruits on top of the cake. Glaze generously with the remaining melted jam and leave to set before serving.

❋ *before decorating* Ⓥ
65^1/$_2$ POINTS values per recipe
263 calories per serving
Serves 16

Potato and spring onion bread

Serve a chunk of this tempting soda bread with a bowlful of soup or stew. Soda bread is best eaten on the day it is made, but it can also be frozen successfully. *Takes 10 minutes to prepare, 40 minutes to cook.*

175 g (6 oz) self raising flour
$^1/_2$ teaspoon bicarbonate of soda
salt and freshly ground black pepper
200 g (7 oz) potato, peeled and grated coarsely
6 spring onions, sliced
3 teaspoons freshly chopped thyme
1 medium egg
2 tablespoons skimmed milk
low fat cooking spray

● Preheat the oven to Gas Mark 5/190°C/ fan oven 170°C.
● Sift the flour, bicarbonate of soda and a pinch of salt into a mixing bowl and season with pepper. Stir the grated potato, spring onions and 2 teaspoons thyme into the flour until evenly mixed.
● Beat the egg with the milk and mix in to form a soft, but not sticky, dough. Shape into a 15 cm (6 inch) round on a baking tray, lightly greased with low fat cooking spray, then mark into six wedges with a knife, but don't cut all the way through to the tray.
● Scatter the remaining thyme over the loaf, then bake in the oven for 40 minutes, or until the loaf is really crisp and sounds hollow when the base is tapped. Cool slightly on a wire rack before eating.

❄ Ⓥ
12$^1/_2$ POINTS values per recipe
143 calories per serving
Serves 6

Squishy squash ginger cake

The grated butternut squash keeps this sponge cake moist. Nuggets of stem ginger add little bursts of flavour. *Takes 20 minutes to prepare, 40–45 minutes to cook.*

low fat cooking spray
200 g (7 oz) self raising flour
1 heaped teaspoon ground ginger
1 teaspoon baking powder
salt
100 g (3^1/$_2$ oz) soft light brown sugar
2 medium eggs, beaten
100 g (3^1/$_2$ oz) low fat polyunsaturated margarine, melted
2 tablespoons skimmed milk
40 g (1^1/$_2$ oz) stem ginger in syrup, drained and diced
175 g (6 oz) butternut squash, grated coarsely
15 g (^{1}/$_2$ oz) flaked almonds

- Preheat the oven to Gas Mark 4/180°C/ fan oven 160°C. Lightly grease a 20 cm (8 inch) round deep cake tin with low fat cooking spray and line it with baking parchment.
- Sift the flour, ginger, baking powder and a pinch of salt into a large bowl. Stir in the sugar then make a well in the centre. Add the beaten eggs, melted margarine and milk, then stir until smooth.
- Mix in the diced ginger and grated squash, then pour into the prepared tin and level the surface. Scatter the almonds on top.
- Bake in the centre of the oven for 40–45 minutes, or until a skewer comes out clean. Cover with baking parchment halfway through the cooking time if the cake is browning too quickly.

- Cool the cake in the tin for 10 minutes before turning out on to a wire rack to finish cooling. Store in an airtight container.

❄ Ⓥ
29^1/$_2$ POINTS values per recipe
188 calories per serving
Serves 10

Golden raspberry buns

A sweet treat to round off a meal, these are a great addition to a packed lunch. *Takes 15 minutes to prepare, 15–20 minutes to cook.*

low fat cooking spray
2 medium eggs, separated
200 g (7 oz) low fat plain yogurt
150 g (5^1/$_2$ oz) Apple sauce (page 22)
100 g (3^1/$_2$ oz) instant dry polenta or cornmeal
3 tablespoons granulated artificial sweetener
salt
^{1}/$_2$ teaspoon cream of tartar
150 g (5^1/$_2$ oz) raspberries

- Preheat the oven to Gas Mark 4/180°C/ fan oven 160°C.
- Mix the egg yolks with the yogurt and apple sauce, then stir in the polenta, sweetener and a pinch of salt.
- In a separate bowl, whisk the eggs whites and cream of tartar to the soft peak stage. Stir a spoonful into the batter to slacken the mixture, then carefully fold in the remainder. Stir in 100 g (3^1/$_2$ oz) raspberries, then spoon the batter into a non stick bun tin lightly greased with low fat cooking spray. Scatter the remaining raspberries on top of each bun.
- Bake for 15–20 minutes until firm, then cool slightly on a wire rack before eating.

NB Only on **Core Plan** if eaten as part of a meal.

❄ Ⓥ
11 POINTS values per recipe
101 calories per serving
Makes 8

chapter ten: **foolproof favourites**

Here are the favourite everyday recipes that you know you can always rely on. The good old-fashioned family staples such as Cottage pie, Lasagne, Chicken casserole and Bangers and mash with roasted onion gravy as well as a delicious Perfect Sunday roast beef. Guaranteed to please, they're a great way to feed the whole family but still ensure that you and your family are eating wisely and maintaining a balanced lifestyle and healthy eating plan.

a great way to
feed the whole family

Chicken casserole

Serve this comforting casserole with some fresh green cabbage, and a jacket potato for an extra **POINTS** value of 2^1/$_2$. *Takes 15 minutes to prepare, 1 hour to cook.*

low fat cooking spray
salt and freshly ground black pepper
4 x 125 g skinless, boneless chicken breast fillets
3 medium leeks, trimmed and thickly sliced
3 medium carrots, peeled and thickly sliced
200 g (7 oz) mushrooms, halved
2 tablespoons plain flour
40 g (1^1/$_2$ oz) pearl barley
1 tablespoon freshly chopped thyme
300 ml (10 fl oz) dry cider

• Lightly coat a casserole dish with low fat cooking spray.
• Season the chicken and brown for 1 minute each side over a high heat, then remove to a plate.
• Add the leeks, carrots and mushrooms to the casserole and fry for 2–3 minutes until lightly coloured.
• Stir in the flour, followed by the pearl barley, thyme, cider and 100 ml (3^1/$_2$ fl oz) water. Season, bring to a simmer and cover.
• Cook gently for 1 hour, or until the vegetables and pearl barley are tender.

❄
13^1/$_2$ **POINTS** *values per recipe*
272 calories per serving
Serves 4

Fish pie

This fish pie has a rosti-style grated potato topping instead of the usual mash. *Takes 30 minutes to prepare, 25 minutes to cook.*

500 g (1 lb 2 oz) smoked haddock
600 ml (1 pint) skimmed milk
2 bay leaves
750 g (1 lb 10 oz) potatoes, roughly the same size
300 g (10^1/$_2$ oz) cooked, peeled prawns
40 g (1^1/$_2$ oz) low fat polyunsaturated margarine
50 g (1^3/$_4$ oz) plain flour
1 tablespoon lemon juice
1 tablespoon freshly chopped parsley
salt and freshly ground black pepper

• Preheat the oven to Gas Mark 4/180°C/fan oven 160°C.
• Place the smoked haddock in a roasting tin, pour in the milk, add the bay leaves, and bake in the oven for 15 minutes or until the fish flakes easily.
• Meanwhile, cook the unpeeled potatoes in water for 8 minutes. Drain and leave to cool slightly.
• Lift the fish on to a plate then break into flakes using a fork, discarding any skin and bones. Transfer to a baking dish and mix with the prawns.
• Place the margarine and flour in a non stick saucepan and gradually blend in the fishy milk. Bring to a simmer, stirring until smooth, then simmer for 3 minutes. Add the lemon juice, parsley and seasoning to taste. Remove the bay leaves and pour into the baking dish.
• Scrape the skins from the potatoes then coarsely grate the potatoes straight over the baking dish to form an even topping.
• Bake for 25 minutes until crisp and golden.

❄ *before cooking*
26 **POINTS** *values per recipe*
423 calories per serving
Serves 4

Steak and mushroom pie

The deeply savoury steak and mushroom filling can be made in advance, then topped with the pastry, and baked for a filling main meal. Perfect with carrots and runner beans. *Takes 20 minutes to prepare, 2 hours to cook the filling, 25 minutes to cook the pie.*

low fat cooking spray
1 onion, sliced
450 g (1 lb) lean beef braising steak, diced
250 g (9 oz) mushrooms, chopped roughly if large
15 g (¹/₂ oz) plain flour
300 ml (10 fl oz) beef stock
salt and freshly ground black pepper
for the pastry
150 g (5¹/₂ oz) plain flour, plus ¹/₂ tablespoon for rolling
65 g (2¹/₄ oz) low fat polyunsaturated margarine
1 tablespoon skimmed milk

● Lightly coat a casserole dish with low fat cooking spray, add the onion and fry over a medium heat for 5 minutes.
● Meanwhile, brown the diced beef in a non stick frying pan over a high heat, in two batches, adding the meat to the casserole as it is done.
● Stir the mushrooms and flour into the casserole, then blend in the stock. Season, bring to a simmer, cover and cook very gently for 2 hours or until the beef is tender.
● Transfer to a lipped ceramic pie dish and cool for at least 10 minutes.
● Preheat the oven to Gas Mark 5/190°C/ fan oven 170°C. While the filling is cooking, make the pastry. Sift the flour and a pinch of salt into a bowl. Add a grinding of black pepper, then rub in the margarine until the mixture is crumbly. Mix in just enough cold water to bring the pastry together

cleanly. Shape into a flat disc, wrap in cling film and chill in the fridge for at least 30 minutes.
● Dust the work surface with ¹/₂ tablespoon flour and roll the pastry out so that it is slightly larger than the pie dish.
● Cut a narrow strip of pastry and press on to the dampened rim of the pie dish. Lift the pastry lid on top and press down around the edges with a fork to seal. Brush with milk, place on a baking tray and cook for 25 minutes until crisp and golden brown.

❋ *filling only*
25¹/₂ POINTS values per recipe
383 calories per serving
Serves 4

Cauliflower cheese

A time-honoured vegetable side dish. *Takes 20 minutes to prepare, 20 minutes to cook.*

1 large cauliflower, broken into florets
2 bay leaves
50 g (1³/₄ oz) low fat polyunsaturated margarine
50 g (1³/₄ oz) plain flour
300 ml (10 fl oz) skimmed milk
300 ml (10 fl oz) vegetable stock
1 teaspoon Dijon mustard
15 g (¹/₂ oz) freshly grated Parmesan
100 g (3¹/₂ oz) mature half fat cheese, grated
salt and freshly ground black pepper
2 spring onions, sliced
15 g (¹/₂ oz) fresh breadcrumbs

● Preheat the oven to Gas Mark 6/200°C/ fan oven 180°C.
● Add the cauliflower florets and bay leaves to a large pan of boiling water. Simmer for 5 minutes until tender, then drain well in a colander. Transfer to an ovenproof dish and discard the bay leaves.
● Place the margarine in a non stick saucepan with the flour, milk and vegetable stock. Bring to the boil, whisking until thickened, then simmer for 3 minutes.
● Remove from the heat and stir in the mustard, Parmesan and 80 g (3 oz) cheese. Season to taste and pour over the cauliflower.
● Mix the spring onions with the breadcrumbs and remaining cheese and scatter over the cauliflower.
● Bake in the oven for 15–20 minutes until browned and crisp.

Ⓥ
16 POINTS values per recipe
245 calories per serving
Serves 4

Bangers and mash with onion gravy

A family favourite with roasted onion gravy *Takes 10 minutes to prepare, 20 minutes to cook.*

1 onion, sliced thickly
4 thick, low fat sausages
1 teaspoon olive oil
salt and freshly ground black pepper
500 g (1 lb 2 oz) potatoes, peeled and diced
5 tablespoons skimmed milk
freshly grated nutmeg
1 tablespoon cornflour
150 ml (5 fl oz) vegetable stock
1 tablespoon tomato ketchup

● Preheat the oven to Gas Mark 6/200°C/ fan oven 180°C.
● Toss the onion and sausages with the oil and seasoning and spread out on a baking tray. Roast in the oven for 10 minutes, then turn the sausages over and stir the onions around. Return to the oven for 5 minutes, then remove the roasted onions to a plate and cook the sausages for 5 more minutes.
● As soon as the sausages and onions go in the oven, add the potatoes to a large pan of boiling water. Cook for about 15 minutes or until tender, then drain.
● Heat the milk in the pan, add the drained potatoes and mash together. Add nutmeg and seasoning to taste.
● While the potatoes are cooking, blend the cornflour with a little of the stock in a non stick saucepan, to make a paste. Mix in the remaining stock and ketchup and simmer for 5 minutes, then add the roasted onions and simmer for a further 2 minutes. Pour the onion gravy over the bangers and mash to serve.

13 POINTS values per recipe
404 calories per serving
Serves 2

Lasagne

A low **POINTS** value version of this classic Italian recipe. Serve with a crisp green salad. *Takes 30 minutes to prepare, 30 minutes to cook meat sauce + 40 minutes to bake the lasagne.*

for the meat sauce
1 onion, chopped finely
500 g (1 lb 2 oz) extra lean minced beef
250 g (9 oz) mushrooms, chopped
3 garlic cloves, crushed
2 teaspoons dried mixed herbs
400 g can chopped tomatoes
300 ml (10 fl oz) beef stock
3 tablespoons tomato purée
salt and freshly ground black pepper

for the white sauce
40 g (1^1/$_2$ oz) low fat polyunsaturated margarine
40 g (1^1/$_2$ oz) plain flour
450 ml (16 fl oz) skimmed milk
150 ml (5 fl oz) vegetable stock
2 bay leaves
freshly grated nutmeg

to assemble
8 sheets dried lasagne
25 g (1 oz) freshly grated Parmesan

● To make the meat sauce, brown the onion and beef mince in a large frying pan over a medium heat for 8 minutes, stirring to break up the meat.
● Mix in the remaining ingredients and seasoning, bring to a simmer and cook, covered, for 20 minutes. Remove the lid and simmer for a further 10 minutes.
● Preheat the oven to Gas Mark 4/180°C/ fan oven 160°C.
● For the white sauce, place the margarine in a non stick saucepan with the flour, milk, stock and bay leaves.

● Bring to a simmer, stirring until smooth, then simmer for 3 minutes. Add grated nutmeg and seasoning to taste, and discard the bay leaves.
● To assemble the lasagne, spoon half of the meat sauce into a large ovenproof dish and top with 4 sheets lasagne.
● Repeat with the rest of the meat sauce and lasagne sheets, then pour the white sauce over the top to cover the pasta.
● Scatter the Parmesan evenly over the lasagne, then bake for 40 minutes until golden brown on the top.

variation For a veggie variation, use Quorn mince and vegetable stock instead.

❋ *before cooking*
36 POINTS *values per recipe*
322 *calories per serving*
Serves 6

Perfect Sunday roast beef with Yorkshires

A wonderful mixture of caramelised vegetables surround this joint of roast beef, absorbing all the flavours as they cook. Accompanied by crisp Yorkshire puddings and gravy, this is a Sunday roast to remember. *Takes 20 minutes to prepare, 1¹/₂ hours to cook.*

1 kg (2 lb 4 oz) joint topside or top rump of beef
salt and freshly ground black pepper
350 g (12 oz) baby carrots
250 g (9 oz) parsnips, peeled and cut into chunks
500 g (1 lb 2 oz) potatoes, peeled and cut into chunks
1 red and 1 white onion, peeled and each cut into 6
    wedges through the root
1 tablespoon clear honey
1 tablespoon grain mustard
for the Yorkshire puddings
60 g (2 oz) plain flour
1 medium egg, beaten
150 ml (5 fl oz) skimmed milk
low fat cooking spray
for the gravy
600 ml (1 pint) beef stock
1¹/₂ tablespoons cornflour, blended with a little cold
    water

● Preheat the oven to Gas Mark 5/190°C/ fan oven 170°C.
● Season the beef and place in a large roasting tin. Roast in the oven for 20 minutes initially.
● Meanwhile, toss the carrots, parsnips, potatoes and onions together with seasoning in a large bowl.
● Make the Yorkshire pudding batter by sifting the flour into a bowl, adding seasoning, then gradually whisk in the egg and milk to form a smooth batter. Transfer to a jug, cover, and leave to stand.
● When the beef has had its initial cooking time, lift it out on to a plate, then tip the vegetables into the tin and stir to coat in the roasting juices.
● Return the beef to the tin, and roast for 30 minutes more, stirring the vegetables around once or twice.
● Mix the honey and mustard together and brush this over the beef, then cook for a final 10 minutes. When the beef is ready, transfer it to a warmed serving platter, cover with foil, and leave to rest.
● Return the vegetables to the oven to cook for 10 minutes, increasing the oven temperature to Gas Mark 7/220°C/ fan oven 200°C. Pop a 12 hole, non stick bun tin in the oven to preheat for 5 minutes.
● When the bun tin is hot, remove from the oven and lightly spray each hollow with low fat cooking spray. Quickly pour the Yorkshire pudding batter into the hollows, then place on the top shelf of the oven and cook for 12–15 minutes until well risen and crisp.
● Once the vegetables are tender and caramelised, lift out to the beef serving platter using a slotted spoon. Spoon any fat out of the roasting tin and pour in the beef stock.
● Place the roasting tin on the hob, using an oven glove to hold it, and bubble for 5 minutes, scraping up the delicious caramelised bits from the bottom of the tin. Mix in the cornflour paste and stir until the gravy has thickened. Transfer to a warmed jug.
● Slice the beef thinly, then serve three medium slices of roast beef per person with two Yorkshire puddings, the vegetables and gravy.

44¹/₂ POINTS values per recipe
377 calories per serving
Serves 6

Chilli bean beef

A quick and easy meal; serve with brown rice or crisp skinned jacket potatoes, for an additional **POINTS** value of 2¹/₂. *Takes 10 minutes to prepare, 20 minutes to cook.*

500 g (1 lb 2 oz) extra lean minced beef
1 onion, finely chopped
1 teaspoon ground cumin
1 teaspoon hot chilli powder
2 garlic cloves, crushed
400 g can chopped tomatoes
420 g can mixed pulses, rinsed and drained
200 ml (7 fl oz) beef stock
1 green and 1 yellow pepper, deseeded and diced
salt and freshly ground black pepper

● Brown the minced beef and onion in a large pan over a medium heat for 8 minutes, stirring to break up the meat.
● Mix in the spices and garlic and cook for 30 seconds, then add the remaining ingredients and seasoning.
● Bring to a simmer and cook, partially covered, for 20 minutes.

❄
*21¹/₂ **POINTS** values per recipe*
264 calories per serving
Serves 4

Cottage pie

A great **Core Plan** version of a family favourite.
Takes 30 minutes to prepare, 20 minutes to cook.

1 kg (2 lb 4 oz) potatoes, peeled and chopped roughly
1 medium leek, trimmed and sliced
500 g (1 lb 2 oz) extra lean minced beef
1 onion, chopped finely
175 g (6 oz) carrots, peeled and diced
150 g (5¹/₂ oz) mushrooms, chopped
300 ml (10 fl oz) beef stock
2 tablespoons tomato purée
1 teaspoon Worcestershire sauce
salt and freshly ground black pepper
50 g (1³/₄ oz) low fat soft cheese
4 tablespoons skimmed milk

● Preheat the oven to Gas Mark 6/200°C/ fan oven 180°C.
● Add the potatoes to a large pan of boiling water and simmer for 15 minutes or until tender. Add the leek for the last 2 minutes of the cooking time.
● While the potatoes are cooking, brown the beef and onion over a medium heat in a large pan for 5 minutes, stirring to break up the mince.
● Mix in the carrots and mushrooms, followed by the stock, tomato purée, Worcestershire sauce and seasoning. Bring to a simmer and cook, covered, for 15 minutes, then pour into an ovenproof dish.
● Drain the potatoes and leeks and mash with the soft cheese, milk and seasoning. Spoon on top of the mince and spread out evenly.
● Bake the cottage pie on a baking tray for 20 minutes or until the topping is crisp and golden.

❄ *before cooking*
*30 **POINTS** values per recipe*
394 calories per serving
Serves 4

Veggie spaghetti bolognese

A favourite Italian recipe, but made with Quorn mince for a vegetarian friendly version. *Takes 15 minutes to prepare, 15 minutes to cook.*

1 onion, finely chopped
low fat cooking spray
150 g (5^1/$_2$ oz) mushrooms, sliced
2 garlic cloves, crushed
salt and freshly ground black pepper
350 g pack Quorn mince
^{1}/$_2$ teaspoon dried mixed herbs
1 tablespoon tomato purée
400 g can chopped tomatoes
250 g (9 oz) spaghetti

• Fry the onion in low fat cooking spray over a medium heat for 5 minutes until softened and lightly browned, adding a splash of water, if needed, to prevent it from sticking.
• Stir in the mushrooms, garlic and seasoning, and cook for a further 2 minutes. Add the Quorn mince, herbs, tomato purée and tomatoes, bring to a simmer and cook for 12–15 minutes.
• Meanwhile, add the spaghetti to a large pan of boiling water and cook for 10–12 minutes until al dente.
• Drain the spaghetti and serve in warmed bowls, with the sauce ladled over the top.

❄ *sauce only* Ⓥ *vegan*
17 POINTS values per recipe
332 calories per serving
Serves 4

Chicken tikka masala

Just right for a Friday night. Serve with 150 g cooked brown rice for a *POINTS* value of 3. *Takes 15 minutes to prepare + 30 minutes marinating, 20 minutes to cook.*

200 g (7 oz) low fat plain yogurt
2 teaspoons curry powder
2 teaspoons tomato purée
salt and freshly ground black pepper
4 x 125 g (4^1/$_2$ oz) skinless boneless chicken breast fillets, diced
for the sauce
1 onion, chopped finely
low fat cooking spray
1 tablespoon curry powder
400 g can chopped tomatoes
150 ml (5 fl oz) chicken stock
2 tablespoons freshly chopped coriander

• Mix the yogurt together with the curry powder, tomato purée and seasoning, then stir in the chicken. Cover and marinate in the fridge for 30 minutes.
• Preheat the grill and place the marinated chicken pieces on the grill rack. Grill for 10–15 minutes until cooked through and lightly charred.
• Meanwhile, cook the onion in low fat cooking spray, over a medium heat, for 5–6 minutes in a covered pan with 2 tablespoons water until softened.
• Stir in the curry powder and cook for 30 seconds, then add the tomatoes and chicken stock. Simmer briskly for 5 minutes, then add the grilled chicken and simmer for a further 5 minutes.
• Stir in the coriander just before serving.

NB use brown rice if you're following **Core Plan**.

10 POINTS values per recipe
199 calories per serving
Serves 4

French roast chicken with boulangère potatoes

French housewives roast their chickens breast-side down, which keeps the white meat deliciously moist and tender. The accompanying slow-cooked potato dish got its name because it used to be baked in the residual heat of the French bakers' ovens, once all the daily bread was done. *Takes 15 minutes to prepare, 1 hour 15 minutes to cook.*

1.75 kg (4 lb) whole chicken
$1/2$ lemon
salt and freshly ground black pepper
1 onion, thickly sliced
150 ml (5 fl oz) chicken stock
1 garlic clove, crushed
2 tablespoons freshly chopped tarragon
low fat cooking spray
for the boulangère potatoes
1 kg (2 lb 4 oz) potatoes, peeled and sliced thinly
1 onion, sliced thinly
300 ml (10 fl oz) skimmed milk
500 ml (18 fl oz) chicken stock
small bunch of watercress, to garnish (optional)

- Preheat the oven to Gas Mark 5/190°C/fan oven 170°C.
- Wipe the chicken inside and out with kitchen paper, tuck the lemon half inside and season with salt and freshly ground black pepper.
- Place the sliced onion in a small roasting tin and sit the chicken on top, breast side down.
- Roast for 45 minutes, then turn the chicken breast side up and cook for a further 20–30 minutes until the chicken is cooked. The juices should run clear when the thickest part of the leg is pierced.
- As soon as the chicken is in the oven, layer the potato and onion slices in a baking dish, lightly greased with low fat cooking spray, seasoning as you go.
- Pour the milk and chicken stock over the potatoes so that they are almost covered, then place a sheet of lightly greased foil on top.
- Bake in the oven for 1–1$1/2$ hours, removing the foil for the last 10 minutes so that the potatoes can brown. The potatoes can be kept warm without spoiling if they are ready before the chicken.
- When the chicken is ready, remove to a platter, cover with foil, and leave to rest for 10 minutes before carving. This will give a juicier, more moist chicken.
- Place the roasting tin on the hob, using an oven glove to hold it, and add the stock, garlic and tarragon. Bring to a simmer, stirring to release the caramelised chicken juices from the tin, and bubble gently for 5 minutes.
- Carve the chicken, removing the skin, and serve with the tarragon gravy and boulangère potatoes. Garnish with some sprigs of watercress if you wish.

*25$1/2$ **POINTS** values per recipe*
415 calories per serving
Serves 4

Lemony roast lamb

This method of roasting lamb on a bed of potatoes is one that is popular in Greece. The potatoes absorb all the flavours as they cook, becoming tender and slightly caramelised. *Takes 10 minutes to prepare, 1 hour 40 minutes to cook.*

1.75 kg (4 lb) leg of lamb
4 garlic cloves, cut into slivers
salt and freshly ground black pepper
2 teaspoons dried oregano
1.2 kg (2 lb 4 oz) potatoes, cut into wedges
300 ml (10 fl oz) lamb or vegetable stock
juice 2 lemons

- Preheat the oven to Gas Mark 5/190°C/ fan oven 170°C.
- Use a small sharp knife to make incisions in the lamb, then press the slivers of garlic into the meat to flavour it as it cooks.
- Season the lamb and rub with half the oregano, then place in a large roasting tin and roast in the oven for 30 minutes.
- Toss the potato wedges with the remaining oregano and seasoning.
- When the 30 minutes is up, briefly lift the lamb out of the roasting tin, tip in the potatoes and turn to coat in the roasting juices.
- Replace the lamb on top of the potatoes, pour the stock into the tin and drizzle the lemon juice all over. Return to the oven and cook for 1 hour, turning the potatoes once or twice.
- Remove the lamb to a carving dish, cover with foil and leave to rest for 10 minutes while the potatoes brown in the oven.
- Carve the lamb, then serve four medium slices of roast lamb per person with the lemony potato wedges.

45$^{1}/_{2}$ POINTS values per recipe
293 calories per serving
Serves 6

Roast pork with baked apples and roast potatoes

Apples baked in the tin alongside the roast pork make for a perfect accompaniment. Serve with a variety of zero vegetables. *Takes 15 minutes to prepare, 2 hours to cook.*

1.5 kg (3 lb 5 oz) boneless pork roasting joint, e.g. loin or leg
salt
6 eating apples, cores removed
1.5 kg (3 lb 5 oz) potatoes, peeled and cut into chunks
1 vegetable stock cube
low fat cooking spray

- Preheat the oven to Gas Mark 7/220°C/fan oven 200°C.
- Season the pork joint with salt and place in a roasting tin. Roast for 15 minutes at the high temperature, then reduce the oven to Gas Mark 5/190°C/fan oven 170°C and cook the pork for a further 1$^{1}/_{2}$ hours, or until the juices run clear.
- Add the apples around the pork for the last 30 minutes, basting them with the cooking juices. Let the pork rest for 15 minutes before carving.
- When the pork has been cooking for 1 hour, cook the potatoes in boiling water, with the vegetable stock cube added, for 10 minutes. Drain, then return to the pan, with the lid on, and shake lightly to roughen up the edges.
- Tip the potatoes into a large roasting tin, lightly coat with low fat cooking spray, and roast at the top of the oven for about 50 minutes, turning halfway through, until crisp and golden.
- Remove the fat from the pork and carve into thin slices. Serve four slices of roast pork per person with the roast potatoes and baked apples.

38$^{1}/_{2}$ POINTS values per recipe
426 calories per serving
Serves 6

Moussaka

Serve this flavoursome classic Greek dish with a crisp green salad. *Takes 35 minutes to prepare, 40 minutes to cook.*

1 aubergine, cut into 1 cm ($^1/_2$ inch) slices
salt and freshly ground black pepper
500 g (1 lb 2 oz) lean lamb mince
1 onion, chopped finely
$^1/_2$ teaspoon dried mint
1 teaspoon cinnamon
500 g carton passata
low fat cooking spray
500 g (1 lb 2 oz) potatoes, peeled and cut into 1 cm
   ($^1/_2$ inch) slices
1 medium egg, beaten
300 g (10$^1/_2$ oz) 0% fat Greek yogurt
freshly grated nutmeg
4 tomatoes, sliced

- Preheat the grill. Lightly salt the aubergine slices to draw out the excess moisture and set aside on a plate for 10 minutes.
- Brown the lamb mince and onion in a large pan over a high heat for about 7 minutes, stirring to break up the meat.
- Mix in the mint, cinnamon, passata and seasoning, then cover and simmer for 5 minutes.
- Pat the aubergine slices dry, mist with low fat cooking spray, and grill for 2–3 minutes each side, until golden.
- Preheat the oven to Gas Mark 6/200°C/ fan oven 180°C.
- Add the potato slices to a large pan of boiling water, stirring gently so that they don't stick together. Simmer for 3–4 minutes, until tender but not falling apart, then drain carefully.
- Spoon half the meat into a baking dish, then cover with half the potatoes. Repeat the meat and potato layers, then cover with the aubergines.

- Mix the egg into the yogurt and add nutmeg and seasoning to taste. Spread over the aubergines, then arrange the tomato slices on top.
- Bake in the oven for 40 minutes until browned and bubbling.

31 POINTS values per recipe
461 calories per serving
Serves 4

Tiramisu

This layered dessert looks impressive when turned out and sliced. *Takes 15 minutes to prepare + chilling.*

2 tablespoons instant coffee
5 tablespoons icing sugar, plus $^1/_2$ teaspoon for
**   dusting**
24 sponge fingers
250 g (9 oz) Quark
250 g (9 oz) very low fat plain fromage frais
1 teaspoon vanilla extract
25 g (1 oz) dark chocolate (70% cocoa), grated
1 teaspoon cocoa powder

- Line a 900 g (2 lb) loaf tin with cling film (brushing the tin with a little water first will help to make the cling film stick).
- Dissolve the coffee and 2 tablespoons icing sugar in 225 ml (8 fl oz) boiling water in a shallow dish. Dip eight sponge fingers in the coffee and press into the base of the loaf tin.
- Whisk the Quark, fromage frais, vanilla and 3 tablespoons icing sugar together until smooth. Spoon half of the mixture into the tin, level out and sprinkle with half the grated chocolate.
- Dip eight more sponge fingers in the coffee and arrange in the tin, then cover with the remaining creamy mixture and chocolate. Finish off with the rest of the sponge fingers, dipped in coffee. Cover with cling film and place a piece of card on top, cut to fit just inside the tin. Weigh down with a couple of cans and chill in the fridge for 4 hours.
- To serve, remove the cans and card, turn out on to a plate, and remove the cling film. Mix the cocoa powder with $^1/_2$ teaspoon icing sugar and dust over the tiramisu. Cut into slices, allowing one sponge finger width per person.

Ⓥ
*19$^1/_2$ **POINTS** values per recipe*
147 calories per serving
Serves 8

White choc chip brownies

Who doesn't love a good brownie? Stored in an airtight container, these chocolate delights will be even more gooey and fudgey the day after baking.
Takes 10 minutes to prepare, 20 minutes to cook.

low fat cooking spray
175 g (6 oz) self raising flour
40 g (1^1/$_2$ oz) cocoa powder
salt
100 g (3^1/$_2$ oz) light muscovado sugar
1 egg, beaten
1 teaspoon vanilla extract
100 g (3^1/$_2$ oz) low fat plain yogurt
80 g (3 oz) low fat polyunsaturated margarine, melted
25 g (1 oz) white chocolate chips

- Preheat the oven to Gas Mark 4/180°C/ fan oven 160°C.
- Lightly grease a 20 cm (8 inch) square cake tin with low fat cooking spray and line it with baking parchment. Sift the flour, cocoa powder and a pinch of salt into a mixing bowl and stir in the sugar.
- Whisk the egg, vanilla and yogurt together with 150 ml (5 fl oz) cold water. Pour into the dry ingredients, add the melted margarine and mix well until smooth.
- Stir in the chocolate chips, then pour the batter into the lined tin.
- Bake the brownies for 20 minutes until they are set and the top is slightly cracked. The brownies should still be slightly sticky in the centre.
- Cool in the tin and cut into 12 pieces. Store in an airtight container.

❄ Ⓥ
29^1/$_2$ POINTS values per recipe
139 calories per serving
Makes 12